HEART INTELLIGENCE

Connecting with the Heart's Intuitive Guidance
for Effective Choices and Solutions

NEW EDITION

Doc Childre, Howard Martin,
Deborah Rozman and Rollin McCraty

Waterside Productions

Printed in the United States of America

First Edition Printing, 2016
Second Edition Printing, 2022

HeartMath is a registered trademark of Quantum Intech, Inc. (dba HeartMath, Inc.) For all HeartMath trademarks go to www.heartmath.com/trademarks

ISBN-13: 978-1-956503-63-0 print edition
ISBN-13: 978-1-956503-64-7 ebook edition

Waterside Productions
2055 Oxford Ave
Cardiff, CA 92007
www.waterside.com

"For centuries the world's greatest teachers have been advising us to follow our heart. Finally we have a simple but powerful book that shows us exactly how to do it. Impeccable scientific research inspired by Doc Childre's deep wisdom about the truth of who we are proves that a few simple heart-centered techniques done consistently over time can transform not only our own lives, but the whole world.
I'm not exaggerating when I say *Heart Intelligence* should be required reading for everybody on the planet."

— **Jack Canfield, Coauthor of *The Success Principles*™ and the NY Times #1 Bestselling *Chicken Soup for the Soul* series**

"*Heart Intelligence* is a wonderful exploration of the science of the deeper heart and why we should learn to listen to it. This book is required reading for anyone who wants to get their heart and head working together to create and *not wait* for their fulfillment."

— **John Gray, Bestselling Author of *Men Are from Mars, Women Are from Venus,* and *Venus on Fire, Mars on Ice***

"The HeartMath Institute has done it once again! By using science as the contemporary language of mysticism, they have elegantly married age old wisdom and spirituality with their latest cutting-edge research and then they provide us with the practical tools to begin our own journey into heart intelligence. This book is an impeccable representation of what we all innately believe to be true. The brain may think, but the heart knows."

— **Dr. Joe Dispenza, NY Times Bestselling Author of You Are the Placebo: *Making Your Mind Matter* and *Breaking the Habit of Being Yourself*: *How to Lose Your Mind and Create a New One.***

"Doc Childre and the HeartMath team have written a powerful book from a place of deep love and care for people. They offer profound insights to access the intuitive intelligence we each need to make our highest choices during these changing times. I believe *Heart Intelligence* will make a big difference in the lives of many people."

— **Lynne Twist, Co-founder, The Pachamama Alliance, author of the award-winning book *The Soul of Money***

"This book is destined to help many people learn how to live from their heart's intuitive guidance to connect the puzzle pieces of their purpose and fulfillment. I love HeartMath and have used its methods to connect with my intuitive heart with great success. In fact, learning to listen to and follow my heart has been the secret to my success."

— **Marci Shimoff, #1 NY Times Bestselling Author,** *Happy for No Reason, Love For No Reason,* **and** *Chicken Soup for the Woman's Soul*

"Heart Intelligence is a fascinating, powerful way to learn how to relieve stress and improve the overall health of your mind and body. I highly recommend it."

— **Daniel Amen, MD, author of the NY Times Mega Bestseller** *Change Your Brain, Change Your Life.*

"Heart Intelligence, is an informative work and an excellent resource to use as a compass in divining the path of your life."

— **Bruce Lipton, PhD., author of** *The Honeymoon Effect* **and of the bestseller** *Biology of Belief.*

"Heart Intelligence is a must read for those wanting to enrich their own lives and our shared experience of life. It unlocks the wisdom and potential within all of us to transform our personal lives, our relationships and the future through profound heart and mind connections. Buy this book for yourself and give copies to those you care about."

— **Simon Mainwaring, CEO We First, author of** *We First*

"Between these covers lies the key to resilience in times of change, uncertainty, and stress. *Heart Intelligence* is a must read."

— **Barnet Bain, director** *Milton's Secret* **(Eckhart Tolle movie to be released fall 2016), producer** *What Dreams May Come,* **author** *The Book of Doing and Being.*

"Heart Intelligence is a must read! For bio-hackers, performance junkies or anyone interested in a better life, the ideas in the book are critical."

— **Steven Kotler, NY Times Bestselling Author of** *The Rise of Superman, Bold and Abundance.*

"*Heart Intelligence: Connecting with the Intuitive Guidance of the Heart*
encourages us to roll our sleeves up and do what we feel we already know
but are too busy to give attention to. This informative book teaches us
how to connect with our heart's intuitive guidance *moment-to-moment*
to make better choices *even* in the middle of challenging situations. It's a
must read."
— **Dr. Ivan Misner, BNI Founder & NY Times Bestselling Author**

"*Heart Intelligence: Connecting With the Intuitive Guidance of the Heart* is
a concise handbook for heart-based living. In a conversational style that's
easy-to-read, the authors lead us on a journey of empowered living — for
us, our families, our communities, and ultimately, for our world. From
engineers to homemakers, from politicians to healers, *Heart Intelligence*
gives new meaning to the role of your heart—while awakening the deep
intuition that can empower the best choices you will ever make. I love this
book!"
— **Gregg Braden, NY Times Bestselling Author of *The Divine Matrix* and
*Resilience From The Heart***

"**Heart Intelligence: Connecting with the Heart's Intuitive Guidance for
Effective Choices and Solutions** is going to help so many people as it's an
easy read and when you're done it's changed you — you're more in your
heart and your heart prompts you. Just by reading this book I'm feeling
heart nudges, heart reminders."
— **Gayle Gladstone, Film and Music Producer**

DEDICATION

This book is dedicated to the increasing numbers of people who are feeling a desire for a deeper connection with their heart. Our mission at HeartMath is to help people bring their physical, mental and emotional systems into coherent alignment with their heart's intelligent guidance system. We feel that establishing this alignment, along with expanding our love, kindness, and compassion, will become the new baseline for people getting along with each other and creating the world as we want it to be. Our research and tools are dedicated to simplifying this process, in cooperation with like-hearted people from around the world who hold important pieces of the puzzle.

CONTENTS

INTRODUCTION

By Doc Childre

The rapid global changes we are experiencing can result in beneficial outcomes for humanity over time, but at this point the planet and humanity seem to be caught in the stress of polarizing biases while worn down by the pandemic. Most of us are experiencing heightened reactions to stress triggers along with understandable anxiety from uncertainty. Part of today's new norm for many is feeling mood swings of hope and encouragement one day, fear, anxiety, or resignation the next.

A 2021 Harris Poll survey on stress and decision-making in America found that more than one-third of adults said it's more stressful to make day-to-day decisions and major life decisions. Despite these struggles, most have retained a positive outlook.[1]

During the pandemic people re-evaluated their priorities and connected with deeper values regarding their relationships with family and work—many became more optimistic about the future as a result. Another 2021 Harris Poll survey reported: "Sweeping research suggests the future is bright and we are rethinking, resetting, and reimagining our futures for the better. Hope and optimism are increasing, connections with friends and family are strengthening and we are re-prioritizing towards what matters to us most."[2]

Caring and genuine heart connections help to offset stress accumulation from anxiety, fear, or panic, while clearing the mind for effective reasoning, especially when confronted with health, financial or societal challenges. Increasing numbers of people throughout the world are feeling a deeper desire to connect with their heart's compassionate care and kindness and have more non-judgmental acceptance of each other. This will soon be realized as highly intelligent and efficient *street sense*. The new spiritual is to bring these qualities of the heart to the street in our day-to-day interactions with each other.

Most of us feel a desire for more harmonious interactions, but we have to step into it with our heart's intention in order to change old hand-me-down habits of separation. We can and will eventually do this. It's *who we are at the core*.

The objective is for humanity to go for sustaining compassion and cooperation without needing stress to motivate us. Solutions are within our hearts. Caring and sharing with each other can do much to increase our connection with the heart's intelligent guidance and solutions. There are many levels of awareness and perceptions throughout humanity. Our minds may be different based on our beliefs, upbringing, and life situations, but we can increase our harmonious interactions with each other once our true heart desires this. Our heart intelligence knows the practical energy efficiency and effectiveness of learning to get along with others. In our deeper heart we can sense that nothing is going to change until we do.

It's in the heart that people access the qualities of love, such as compassion, care, kindness, forgiveness, and appreciation that lift us above separation, judgments, and blame. Through intentionally demonstrating these heart qualities in our lives, we connect with our heart's natural intelligence and intuitive guidance for a unique opportunity to create a future together in harmony. Yes, it takes a little attention and energy to practice these heart qualities, but not as much as it takes to recoup from stress, health and relationship problems that accrue from not including our heart's guidance in our interactions and choices.

The guiding feelings and nudges from our heart have been referred to in teachings throughout millennia. Unlocking this inner guidance enables us to navigate through changing and chaotic times with more balance, coherence, and heart-based connections with each other. Doing this can help shift humanity's energies from separation to cooperation, resulting in higher solutions to our global, social, and economic problems.

One of our goals in writing this book is to help clarify how each person's heart intelligence (heart's intuitive guidance) can help us connect to our higher choices and untapped potentials for creating what's best for us. Learning to establish coherence between our mind, heart, and emotions expands our love and compassionate care. Increasing the love flowing through our system is one of the best kept secrets for connecting with our heart's intuitive directions. Following our heart unfolds the essence of *who we truly are*, which leads to our happiness and fulfillment. HeartMath research and tools have been designed to simplify and facilitate this process.

The HeartMath mission is to research and create heart-based tools and helpful exercises, and then to work in alignment with other systems and organizations to increase harmony, compassion and well-being throughout the planet. Many people have so much to offer during these times.

HeartMath tools and techniques are designed to be used in the moment and *on-the-go*. Our focus is to create tools that don't require a lot of time or long meditations. We way respect meditation and do longer heart meditations ourselves to broadcast love and compassion out to the planet. However, with the rise in stress, people don't have time to meditate each time a challenging situation comes up. Most of the tools in this book can be used on the spot as needed once you get familiar with them. But at first, it does take focus to intentionally practice the tool for a week or so to imprint it in memory. Then it's easier to have a natural tendency to use the tool when needed.

This new edition of *Heart Intelligence* has been updated for today's challenging and changing times. It provides an overview of HeartMath Institute's research on personal, social, and global coherence and their applications in the world. A few of our themes include: what is physiological coherence and why it's important; heart-brain synchronization; how heart intuition differs from other types of intuition; increased connection with true self; compassion and self-compassion; transforming fear; aligning with our purpose; and how to clear old energetic habits and imprints that no longer serve us.

This book is written from the tone of our research and each author's practiced experience. Some of the content discusses information that's familiar to many. Yet, a refresher on these subjects is often beneficial for re-boosting our commitments to changing our blocks and resistances to becoming the best of who we can be. Empowerment increases as we access and follow our own heart's intelligence and intuitive guidance. This enables us to become our true self—with the heart power and effectiveness of our love to help change the world. Together, we can co-create a new normal—a world in which it's common sense to be benevolent and to cooperate with each other for the highest good of all.

Doc Childre

HeartMath Founder

January 2022

NOTES:

1. *Stress in America*^{TM} *2021: Stress and Decision-Making during the Pandemic* https://www.apa.org/news/press/releases/stress/2021/october-decision-making

2. *Study Shows New Priorities For Compassion, Community And Career—And A Bright Future by Tracy Brower, Forbes Magazine.* https://www.forbes.com/sites/tracybrower/2021/10/10/study-shows-new-priorities-for-compassion-community-and-career-and-a-bright-future/?sh=421a62d56e38

CHAPTER 1

HEART-BASED LIVING

By Doc Childre

My intention in this book is to provide research and understandings about the "heart" as a dynamic, unifying, creative intelligence. A coherent alignment between our spiritual heart, mind, and emotions can lead to a new way of perceiving, thinking, and relating, we call *heart-based living*.

Heart-based living is a natural self-maintenance, self-transformational practice. It creates a foundation for people learning to get along with each other and work together in harmony, with increased care and cooperation for the best outcome for the wholeness. This begins with befriending the intuitive guidance within our heart and bringing it forward into how we conduct our life day-to-day.

With genuine practice, we *can* find within our heart, personal guidance and directions for the next steps along our path to becoming our empowered, true self. Our heart's intelligence can offer us, personally and collectively, a chance to create (not wait for) our fulfill-ment. Our heart's intuitive feelings and discernments regarding life's issues are natural gifts we can refer to, no matter what personal growth, religion, or spiritual path we may believe in or practice. We don't have to be on a particular path to experience the limitless benefits of our heart's intelligent directions. My approach is that of *practical spirituality*—which includes the practice of integrating heart qualities such as love, kindness, and compassion into our daily interactions with others and allowing for differences without creating separation.

The accelerating changes of these times offer us increased opportunities to advance in consciousness—by integrating our spiritual heart's wisdom with our normal intelligence into a *oneness* relationship. These times are lit with positive opportunity, regardless of how it can appear throughout the planet. The pandemic helped more of humanity to realize we are all connected, and that caring for others and ourselves is caring for the whole. More people are being prompted from within to be kinder to each other. Many are talking about and practicing compassion. There are compassion courses at universities. At the same time, there are healthcare workers and first responders who are feeling compassion fatigue and burnout because of the extreme challenges in caring for others. It's a good time for more of us to send our compassionate care to people in these situations because it's *us* they are looking out for.

Increasingly, people are becoming more sensitive to their heart's promptings to care more, not just for the sake of being good but because it harmonizes the energetic environment. Many are practicing meditation to find inner stillness and to release identification with thoughts and attitudes that no longer serve who they want to become. Increasing numbers are exploring a deeper connection with their heart's feelings and guidance for the reason that nothing else seems to fulfill certain empty spaces in their life. They are sensing that the heart is a natural conduit to their highest love and assistance.

As collective consciousness increases, this will eventually reveal that *love* is an advanced mode of intelligent living. What I mean by *love* is simply more care, kindness, and cooperation in our interactions, along with less judgment, more compassion, and forgiveness. My intention is to give a picture of how love includes these practical and effective ways to heal separation and bitterness between people, which is driving the steady increase in intractable stress that humanity is experiencing. For many of us, it would be safe to say that one of love's principal intentions is to help people get along with each other, which unfolds the secret of thriving and experiencing less fear and more joy.

Creating Hope for the Future

Love generates hope, and hope is a window to future possibilities that serve the highest good for the whole. Often, the light in our hope dims and is obscured by chaos and our own mental and emotional blocks, such as fear, judgment and prejudice. As we practice heart qualities like love, care and cooperation, along with becoming more responsible for our personal energy expenditures, we can become architects of a new sense of hope and live according to deeper values and higher quality choices. As we become more compassionate, more forgiving, and more eager to put the past behind us, this will draw more hopeful and intelligent solutions for the many seemingly insurmountable challenges we are experiencing.

Building trust in our heart's intuitive guidance leads to uplifting possibilities and the increased capacity to manifest them, along with many other upturns we've long hoped for. As our hearts open more to each other, this creates a constant renewal of our sense of hope and optimism for the future. Hope is important but it's time to start *creating* along with it, and not just wait for hope to put solutions on our doorstep. A good first start is to begin expressing more care and compassion and bringing it to the street in our day-to-day interactions as the needed groundwork, then the rest will unfold. Doing this can get easier than not doing it, once we break through the inertia accumulated from our old predictable patterns and reactions. We were born to love, respect, and cooperate with each other, and collective humanity is starting to move in that direction (although it doesn't seem like it at this time).

I feel that we are in a transitional period and this won't last forever. It obviously will go on for a good while until more of us decide to open our hearts to compassionate care and create a different world from what we've created thus far. Eventually our hearts will have had enough of the old and want to pioneer these new changes.

People have just scratched the surface of awareness regarding the focused power of love and its capacity to create a heart-based environment—one where individuals can progressively transform fear and the debilitation it brings, while manifesting their undiscovered gifts and fulfillment. Many are sensing that collective compassionate care is emerging to become the next level of love that humanity is transitioning into. This transition is calling for *heart-based* choices.

The upside is there is a growing momentum of more and more people committing to heart-directed choices, realizing their practical effectiveness for reducing stress, staying balanced and in charge through rapidly shifting times. Learning to access our heart's intelligence for discerning choices and directions will eventually be accepted as common sense. Heartfelt interactions between our own mind and emotions and with each other is the foundation for people of different races, religions, politics, and beliefs to get along harmoniously. As more of humanity practices heart-based living (or heart-first living), it will help qualify the "rite of passage" into the next level of collective intelligence.

The healing of separation is essential for a shift into the next level of intelligence for humanity—and many people are feeling that life is shaking us awake to this requirement. The increasing influence of a collective heart opening will help dissipate separation and conflict between people and nations. Our present global situation is not the same as a storm where we bunker down and wait 'til it's over, then go back to business as usual. The ball is in our court, as we are all players in the outcome. The global intensities won't last forever. For now, we can view the chaos and unrest as neon signs which indicate it's time to open our hearts, grab our toolbox, and make some needed changes for the better. In doing so, we are repurposing the global stress and uncertainty into a positive momentum to get us off the couch. A deeper commitment to interactive kindness and compassionate latitude stand to become the new baseline for increased coherence, harmony, and cooperation between our own heart and mind, with each other, and with Earth.

CHAPTER 2

IT'S HEART TIME

By Howard Martin

Most of us feel that our lives keep speeding up. That's actually been going on for a while. It just feels like it's going faster now than ever before—more to do in less time, more things pulling us in different directions. It's easy to feel relentlessly bombarded with "high-speed" communications and an overload of information. New technologies designed to make things happen more quickly seem to be quickening us on the inside too. It's often hard to keep up. One word describes what many of us frequently feel—*overwhelmed*.

However, another momentum is also taking place. Many people from different backgrounds, cultures, and professions are sensing an impetus for positive change within themselves and in the world. There is an inner stirring, a prompting from our intuition to awaken to new possibilities and a desire to grow. When I speak to audiences all over the world, I observe people responding to these inner promptings and making changes in the most elegant and beautiful ways. They are taking action on their insights, shifting beliefs and values, overcoming old patterns, accepting and embracing change, and making an effort to facilitate the larger whole.

The increasing complexity we experience in modern life is an outward reflection of the speed of change. Life, including each of us, is always evolving. It is just happening at a very fast pace now, during an important and unique time in history. Old systems are dying and new ones are trying to emerge. Numerous societies and governments are in a state of rapid, often chaotic transformation. Faster change and growth seem to be the evolutionary imperatives of our time.

One of the most important aspects of the changes taking place is the emergence of a more heart-based awareness or "heart intelligence." Learning to access the heart's intelligence is a key to managing the speed of personal and planetary change while creating a new life experience of increased fulfillment. Throughout this book we will explore heart intelligence, what it is, the scientific research on it, how we can develop it, and what can happen as more and more people awaken to this powerful resource that lives within us all.

In the workshops I give, people often share their challenges trying to manage so much change taking place in such a short amount of time. They also share a deep sense of opportunity to help usher in a new and very different world, and the realization that we have to do it together. I am often asked questions such as: *How can we advance personal growth and improve the state of the world? How do we handle so much change and maintain balance? How can we use this momentum of change to find new fulfillment in life? How can we find solutions to problems that seem to have no viable solutions? What can I/we do?* In the forty plus years I've spent focusing on my own personal development, I found that my answers to questions such as these have come from a deep place in my heart, not from mental speculations.

I have been fortunate. When I was a young man I had a realization that life was about continuous growth and I felt my life had to be about service to others in some way. While it was exciting to have these insights, it was also a bit disconcerting. I was overly ambitious, full of myself, and prone to the pitfalls most of us experience as we mature. I pondered how I could stay committed to my growth, make changes I knew I needed to make, and not become complacent. I wondered how I could overcome the resistances, vanities and self-centeredness I had, as well as the growth challenges life can present while trying to find practical, meaningful ways to serve others.

Through pursuing this path with friends and the promptings of life, I began to see that my way forward was through the conscious development of qualities born from what I understood as "heart," such as care and compassion, and replacing judgmental reactiveness with more kindness. My heart's promptings cultivated a genuine desire to become a self-empowered person and to find ways to live that were more balanced, loving, and fulfilling. Following those heart promptings eventually led me to work with Doc Childre and others to help unfold the HeartMath system that Doc was creating.

The development and growth of HeartMath has far exceeded any vision I could possibly have had when we started. That realization alone is something for me to always appreciate. It is verification that life can exceed expectations when I listen to and follow my heart. The practice of unfolding my heart intelligence is what has given me the sustained motivation to stay true to my commitments and put me in a position where I can help others learn how to do this as well.

Simply put, HeartMath is a system for awakening and developing our heart's intelligence. It includes heart-based tools designed to help people self-empower, to connect with their heart's intuitive guidance, and unlock the potential of who they really are. We share the HeartMath system through books, technologies, and training programs that have been delivered to thousands of individuals interested in personal growth or improving their health and performance. HeartMath has worked with Fortune 500 companies, healthcare systems, and social service sectors, such as educational institutions, the military, and law enforcement. Through this process, millions of lives have been touched. We have learned a lot about people, and especially ourselves, some of which we will share in these writings.

As you will find in the coming chapters, science has always played a big role in HeartMath. Long before the HeartMath organizations were officially formed, Doc realized that if we were going to offer a system called "heart intelligence," we needed a bridge to take the philosophical and spiritual understanding of heart into practical day-to-day applications. He chose science as one of the building blocks for that bridge.

When something is better understood through scientific research, it increases the power of belief and application. Many people want to believe in and trust their hearts more, but often don't know the difference between what their heart is saying and their mental or emotional biases. If scientific research could reveal new understandings about the heart, emotions, and mind, it would make it easier for people to accept and apply what they already intuitively know and feel.

In the early 1990s the HeartMath Research Center was established, and since that time it has greatly expanded people's understanding of the heart's role beyond being just an organ that pumps our blood. In forthcoming chapters you will see that the heart is also an information processing center that sends important messages throughout the body and can have profound influences on our brain. In the lab, our researchers started by looking at the physiological connection between emotional states, the heart, and the brain. They found that a measurement called heart rate variability (HRV) is reflective of people's emotional states and that HRV or heart rhythm analysis offers a unique window into the communication between the heart, brain, and emotions.[1] Over the years, the HeartMath Research Lab has become one of the leading authorities in this field.

Researching HRV has helped us refine techniques to improve heart/brain communication and to self-generate a highly beneficial physical and emotional state called physiological coherence, or "heart coherence" for short. We found that positive feelings of love, care, appreciation, and other uplifting emotional qualities long-associated with heart activated this state of coherence. This important discovery on the link between emotion and the heart's rhythms was published in the *American Journal of Cardiology* in 1995 and then in other peer-reviewed scientific journals.[2] Further studies on how people can learn to activate heart coherence led to the development of our HRV technology products (originally Freeze-Framer™, then emWave®, and Inner Balance™ Trainer), which by now have been used by people in more than 100 countries as a way of training themselves to improve their emotional self-regulation and self-empowerment skills.

Social science has also played a role in our research. We created pre- and post-assessments to determine the effectiveness of our programs in organizations, healthcare, and education. We found that as people practice HeartMath methods, there are significant results in lowered stress levels, improved health, reduced healthcare costs, improved test scores, and heightened ability to sustain positive emotional states, along with other performance measures. Increased heart coherence also results in a deeper connectedness between people. Researchers recorded a number of instances in which a loving mother's brain waves synchronized to her baby's heartbeats and where happy couples' heart rhythms synchronized with each other when sleeping together.[3] They also found that increased physiological heart coherence in individual team members resulted in enhanced synchronization and performance—a type of team coherence.

Anyone who has watched a championship sports team or experienced an exceptional concert knows that something special can happen in a group that transcends their normal performance. It seems as though the players are in sync and communicating on some unseen energetic level. Many teams, including Olympic and professional sports teams, understand the importance of team coherence. While they may refer to this as "team spirit" or "bonding," they instinctively know there is a palpable "team energy" that impacts their performance. Such elite teams pay close attention to their group's cohesion, and the team leaders actively take steps to resolve any interpersonal conflicts or distortions that may hinder or erode it. They know that internal group discord or conflict has a negative impact on the team. They also know it takes connecting with the power of the heart to create team coherence.

Curt Cronin, CDR (SEAL), a former commander of Navy SEAL Team Six and his partner Dr. Jay Ferraro, PhD, are HeartMath Certified Trainers who work with NFL players and teams using HeartMath techniques with emWave HRV technology to help them connect with the power of the heart and monitor their heart rhythms to develop team coherence. Here is great story that illustrates what can happen when a higher level of team coherence occurs. It was taken from the book, *Second Wind: The Memoirs of an Opinionated Man* written by basketball legend Bill Russell.

"Every so often a Celtics game would heat up so that it became more than a physical or even mental game, and would be magical. That feeling is difficult to describe, and I certainly never talked about it when I was playing. When it happened, I could feel my play rise to a new level. It came rarely, and would last anywhere from five minutes to a whole quarter, or more. Three or four plays were not enough to get it going. It would surround not only me and the other Celtics, but also the players on the other team, and even the referees.

"At that special level, all sorts of odd things happened: The game would be in the white heat of competition, and yet somehow I wouldn't feel competitive, which is a miracle in itself. I'd be putting out the maximum effort, straining, coughing up parts of my lungs as we ran, and yet I never felt the pain. The game would move so quickly that every fake, cut, and pass would be surprising, and yet nothing could surprise me. It was almost as if we were playing in slow motion. During those spells, I could almost sense how the next play would develop and where the next shot would be taken. Even before the other team brought the ball inbounds, I could feel it so keenly that I'd want to shout to my teammates, 'it's coming there!'—except that I knew everything would change if I did. My premonitions would be consistently correct, and I always felt then that I not only knew all the Celtics by heart, but also all the opposing players, and that they all knew me. There have been many times in my career when I felt moved or joyful, but these were the moments when I had chills pulsing up and down my spine.

"... On the five or ten occasions when the game ended at that special level, I literally did not care who had won. If we lost, I'd still be as free and high as a sky hawk."

Most all of us have had the experience of walking into a room and feeling immediately uplifted by the positive vibration of the people there, and at another time walking into a room and sensing that people's feelings were at odds with each other although everyone appeared fine. What we were experiencing was some type of heart-to-heart bio-communication or energetic transfer. To research this, the HeartMath team wanted to see if they could detect heart-to-heart bio-communication between a person and their pet.[4]

They looked at the heart rhythms of a twelve-year-old boy, Josh, and his dog, Mabel, using two portable HRV recorders, one fitted on Josh and the other on Mabel. They synchronized the recorders and placed Mabel in one of our labs. Josh then entered the room and sat down a few feet away from Mabel and proceeded to consciously radiate feelings of love towards the dog without touching her. In the graph on the next page note the synchronous shift to increased coherence in the heart rhythms of both Josh and Mabel as Josh consciously radiated love to his dog. An energetic transfer was taking place through their emotional connection. The graph was like a signature that reflected the love and bonding that was taking place.

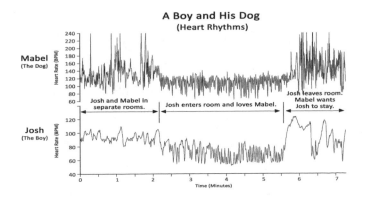

A Boy and His Dog
(Heart Rhythms)

The research lab did a similar experiment with a woman named Ellen and her horse, Tonopah, and saw the same synchronous shift to increased coherence in Ellen and her horse. This occurred while Ellen was practicing HeartMath's Heart Lock-In® technique and sending love to Tonopah *(see graph below)* from just inside the corral. Again both Ellen and her beloved horse were linked in some unseen way.[4]

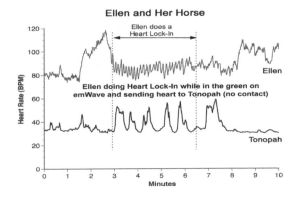

Ellen and Her Horse

When I show these slides in my presentations, people in the audience sometimes start to tear up a little. It touches something deep inside the heart. I know it did with me the first time I saw the graphs. From this research, we can see that as people practice heart coherence, it generates an energetic field that makes it easier for others to connect with their heart and create social coherence.

Today much of our research is focused on the science of interconnectivity. Our vision is to help create a more heart-connected world and to explore the potential of global coherence. It's well-documented that humans and animals are affected by changes in the earth's magnetic (energetic) fields. The research team is testing the hypothesis that humanity is actually interacting with the earth's magnetic fields. Thus far, our research studies have found that the heart rate variability (HRV) or heart rhythms of individuals in different locations across the planet actually synchronized with each other over a 30-day period, indicating humanity is synchronized to rhythms in the earth's fields. (We will talk more about exciting social and global coherence research later in this book.)

Emerging Heart Awareness

There is much more to the emergence of new heart awareness than what HeartMath science or anyone's science has contributed so far. It's in the air. More speakers, articles, books, and programs are referring to the heart. More company mission statements make a point to mention the importance of the heart in leadership and customer care. Whether people mention speaking from the heart, listening to the heart, connecting with the heart, or following the heart, it is a clear sign that there is an increased energetic awareness of the importance of the heart in life's decisions.

I have been seeing more references to the heart and qualities associated with the heart in areas I wouldn't have imagined. For example, in advertising and business. Whether or not it is a motivation to sell more products, advertisers are more overtly using words and images related to heart with messages about love, care, and compassion. "Purpose Driven Marketing" and "Conscious Capitalism" are examples of heart-based movements that are changing how business is done.

A new understanding of heart that moves past just the philosophical, often soft characterization, is advancing into a realization of the heart as a connecting, creative intelligence. Connecting the physical, emotional, intuitive, and spiritual aspects of heart in a coherent alignment can lead to a new way of perceiving, thinking, and acting, which we call heart intelligence.

The purpose of this book is to provide an understanding of heart intelligence and how to apply it in practical ways to raise our vibration, which enables us to manage our energy, unfold our higher potentials, and create a fulfilling life. We will be sharing key practices and concepts, some of which may be new to you and others you may have explored along your own personal path. We will expand on the benefits of learning to access our heart's discernment and guidance to create forward movement through these transformational times with much more clarity, ease, and grace.

Of course, paradigms don't change overnight, but as the planetary heart energetics increase and we gain more understanding of heart intelligence, we will collectively refine and advance the process. As I travel in the US, Europe, and Asia, I see people from many different occupations increasingly demonstrating the qualities of heart intelligence. It's hard to quantify, but amidst the conflicts and struggles taking place I perceive new awareness and hope manifesting. It shows up in casual, uncalculated moments. There is often a different quality in how people communicate with one another, demonstrated by a spirit of openness, general respect, and collaboration. I observe a new alignment with core values that people are using to guide their decisions and actions. It is especially evident in the ways that people react or don't react to challenges. The normal, predictable, emotional patterns just don't seem to be as dominant at times.

The next few paragraphs are some of Doc's thoughts on the planetary shift we are experiencing that helped explain to me what I was seeing.

"Even as the world is becoming more heart-connected, it is also obvious that the global stress bar is being raised. Waves of emotional turbulence modulate throughout the planet, resulting from our collective emotional responses to terrorism, wars, viruses, climate change swings of droughts, floods, tornados and other earth changes, world stage instability, and on. These stress waves get powerfully stirred and amplified by the media, which sustains a collective uneasiness that can dampen how we think, feel, and respond to life's challenges—especially on the emotional level.

"On the upside, the media and internet provide us with a world view that is drawing out more love, care and compassion for humanity's hardships than we've ever experienced at one time on the planet. This influence is showing up in the thousands of social causes that continue to form through the internet connectivity available today. More people are caring and taking action in areas of global challenge like racial, social, and financial inequities, healthcare and political reform, ecology, and much more. The people's voice, the voice of their hearts, is rising and increasingly being heard. People in every part of the world regardless of culture, age, spiritual/religious beliefs, and so on are experiencing an up-grade in heart-based awareness.

"As more people access their heart's intelligence, it creates an energetic connection that makes it easier for others to do the same. We contribute to this energetic momentum of heart-based awareness as we take responsibility to release judgments and separation. This helps to clear the energetic density between our spirit and humanness that restricts the manifestation of our higher potentials. It requires self-empowerment and there is more facilitation and capacity to do that now than ever.

As time unfolds, the general tone of collective consciousness will progressively change from survive to thrive as humanity becomes kinder, more compassionate, and cooperative through this transformational adventure."

It's an adventure in discovering the power of the heart.

NOTES:

1. McCraty, R., Atkinson, M., Tomasino, D., & Bradley, R. T, *The coherent heart: Heart-brain interactions, psychophysiological coherence, and the emergence of system-wide order. Integral Review,* 2009. **5**(2): p. 10-115.

2. McCraty, R., et al., *The effects of emotions on short-term power spectrum analysis of heart rate variability. Am J Cardiol,* 1995. **76**(14): p. 1089-93.

3. McCraty, R., *The energetic heart: Bioelectromagnetic communication within and between people, in Bioelectromagnetic Medicine,* P.J. Rosch and M.S. Markov, Editors. 2004, Marcel Dekker: New York. p. 541-562.

4. McCraty, R., *The Energetic Heart: Biomagnetic Communication Within and Between People, in Bioelectromagnetic and Subtle Energy Medicine, Second Edition,* P.J. Rosch, Editor 2015.

CHAPTER 3

ATTRIBUTES OF HEART INTELLIGENCE

By Deborah Rozman

"Picture heart intelligence as the flow of awareness, understanding, and intuitive guidance we experience when the mind and emotions are brought into coherent alignment with the heart. This intelligence steps down the power of love from universal source into our life's interactions in practical, approachable ways which inform us of a straighter path to our fulfillment."

— Doc Childre

There are many aspects to heart intelligence that we'll touch on from different angles throughout this book. Most people reference their heart as something more than just their physical heart. When I was teaching meditation to children in a public school classroom of seven year olds, I asked them, "Point to your real self," and everyone in the class pointed to their heart. They naturally felt their heart was who they really are. Regardless of race, religion, or ethnicity, throughout history people have referred to their heart as their source of being, intuition, and wisdom. In most every language, we find metaphors of the heart like, "listen to your heart," "go to your heart for the answer," or "put your heart into it." Many ancient cultures, including the Mesopotamians, Egyptians, Babylonians, and Greeks referred to the heart as a source of *intelligence*. They maintained that the heart is the primary organ capable of influencing and directing one's emotions, morality, and decision-making ability, so they consequently attached enormous emotional and moral significance to its behavior. Over thousands of years, most often without knowing about one another, cultures across the planet have seemed to share a similar knowledge about the *heart* as a source of intelligence and inner guidance.

From my personal experience teaching Gestalt psychology to adult classes in the early 1970s, I realized that the head and the heart were two different intelligence systems. There was nothing I could find in the psychological literature at that time that could explain what I was observing. When a student was in conflict about a relationship or career issue, I would place two pillows on the floor and have them pretend one pillow was the head and the other was the heart. I would have students sit on the head pillow and have their head talk to their heart. After sharing their thoughts and concerns, I'd have them move to the heart pillow and tell their head what their heart's view of the problem was and what their heart was feeling. It was often like two different people talking from two different reference points of awareness. Then I'd have them go back to the head pillow and respond to their heart.

After switching pillows in this way three or four times, they'd settle in their heart and speak from their heart's wisdom. What occurred was an obvious shift in the depth of what they would say and a different energetic quality that was palpable to them and the whole class. The intuitive insights that emerged from bringing their head and heart together resulted in a solution to their conflict or a clear next step. I witnessed this so many times I was convinced that the heart was accessing a source of intelligence.

When I met Doc Childre in the mid 1980s and heard him talk about heart intelligence, I immediately knew what he meant, though I wasn't familiar with the term. He invited me and others to help create an institute to explore heart intelligence through research. I accepted the offer with enthusiasm because it resonated with my past studies and experience with the heart.

As we started our research we asked ourselves, *Are the spiritual and physical heart connected in any measurable way? Is what people refer to as heartfelt emotions just an aspect of the brain or is the physical heart involved in emotional experience? Is it involved in intuition?* These are some of the queries we pondered as we formed the HeartMath Research Center in the early 1990s. It was important to understand how the heart and brain communicate and to investigate the heart's role in emotional experience, intuition, and self-regulation. So we formed a scientific advisory board of esteemed brain researchers, cardiologists, psychiatrists, psychologists, physicists, and engineers who were all interested in researching any connection between the physical heart and the spiritual heart.

Our research began with exploring the latest findings in the fields of neuroscience, neuro-cardiology, psychology, physiology, biochemistry, and biophysics. In synthesizing research from these different disciplines, it was surprising to discover that the physical heart sends information to the brain and body through at least four different pathways: neurological communication (through ascending pathways in the autonomic nervous system); bio-physical communication (the pulse wave); biochemical messaging (the heart secretes a number of hormones); and, through the electromagnetic field created by the heart.[1] We also discovered that what we *feel* influences and is influenced by the activity of the physical heart and that our *feelings* are a key aspect to unlocking heart intelligence.

Understanding Intelligence

The word intelligence comes from the Latin verb *intelligere*, which means to "pick out" or discern. This term "intelligence" has a long history of being linked to metaphysical ideas, including theories of the immortality of the soul.[2] However, exploring intelligence was relatively uncommon until the early 1900s. Since then, intelligence has been described in many ways, including our abilities for abstract thought, understanding, self-awareness, communication, reasoning, learning, emotional knowledge, memory retention, planning, and problem-solving. It's interesting that as human awareness has evolved, so have our discernments on what intelligence is.

Today, there are numerous definitions of intelligence by scholars with no real consensus. Within many circles, the definition of intelligence has been limited to the results of the IQ (Intelligence Quotient) test. There has been much criticism of confining a person's intelligence to what can be measured by an IQ test. Critics do not dispute the fact that these tests can predict certain types of achievement rather well. But, they argue, to base our entire concept of human intelligence on IQ scores alone is to ignore many other important aspects of our abilities.[3]

In 1983, Howard Gardner suggested in his book *Frames of Mind* that people have multiple intelligences: logical, linguistic, spatial, musical, kinesthetic, intrapersonal (knowing yourself), naturalist, and interpersonal (knowing others).[4] This opened educators' thinking about intelligence and some schools began to teach to these different intelligences. From there a series of expanded views of intelligence evolved.

In 1995, Daniel Goleman wrote the groundbreaking book, *Emotional Intelligence*, which sparked a new movement, one that took emotions out of the closet and put them on the forefront of awareness. Goleman's exhaustive review of the research into the nature of emotions and intelligence revealed that our success in life is based as much or more on our ability to manage our emotions than on our intellectual or analytical capabilities. He found that our ability to self-regulate and direct our emotions is critical for success in a wide range of occupations, and for building and maintaining friendships.[5]

Goleman's work helped to spawn a new field of scientific inquiry called "positive psychology" based on research findings that positive emotional states actually broaden our thinking. Barbara Fredrickson's "broaden and build" theory describes how negative emotions can't get you into states that enable you to appreciate multiple points of view or facilitate problem-solving and creativity. Only positive emotional states like gratitude and love can do that.[6] Now researchers are talking about a positive "collective intelligence" as human communities evolve towards higher orders of complexity and harmony.

When we began our research on heart intelligence, we had subjects practice heart-focused breathing techniques while generating feelings of appreciation, love, care, or compassion. They frequently reported experiences of heightened intuition and insight for more effective choices in daily living. This gave us reason to suspect that heart-focused practices stimulated our intelligence beyond our normal range of perception. We understood that many sages and philosophers have talked about an intuitive intelligence that provides direct perception and clarity independent of the mind's reasoning processes. But we wanted to also understand the physiological pathways, so our next step was to look at how the heart and brain communicate.

Heart-Brain Research

In-depth research into the physiology of heart-brain communication began in the second half of the twentieth century. During the 1960s and '70s, pioneer physiologists John and Beatrice Lacey conducted research that showed the heart actually communicates with the brain in ways that greatly affect how we perceive and react to the world around us.[7, 8]

In 1991, the year that the HeartMath Institute was established, pioneering neuro-cardiologist Dr. J. Andrew Armour introduced the term "heart brain."[9] He found that the heart possessed its own complex intrinsic nervous system that acts as a brain and functions *independently* from the brain in the head. This heart-brain has been shown to sense, process, and encode information internally. There is evidence that the heart's brain possesses the capacity to learn, and even has short- and long-term memory and neural plasticity. Moreover, ascending neurological signals sent from the heart to the brain continuously interact with and modify the activity in the brain's higher cognitive and emotional centers.[10]

In this way, input originating in the heart is a major and consistent influence in the very processes underlying our perception, cognition, and emotion. At the physical level, the heart not only possesses an innate form of intelligence, but, through its extensive communication with the brain and body, the heart is intimately involved in how we think, feel, and respond to the world.[1]

Today, scientists have learned a great deal more about the heart's independent and intelligent functions, which is still not common knowledge for many people, even clinicians and other researchers. Here are some of the findings:

- The heart starts beating in the unborn fetus before the brain has formed.

- There is constant two-way communication between the heart and brain.

- The heart sends more information to the brain than the brain sends to the heart.

- The heart sends signals to the brain which help inform our choices.

- The heart helps synchronize many systems in the body so that they can function in harmony with one another.

- The heart's signals especially affect the brain centers involved in strategic thinking, reaction times, and self-regulation.

Emotional Self-Regulation

In the early '90s, the HeartMath Research Center found that negative or stressful emotions throw the nervous system out of sync, and when that happens our heart rhythms become disordered and appear jagged on a heart rhythm monitor.[11] This places increased stress on the physical system and negatively impacts mental functions. Positive emotions like appreciation, love, care, and compassion, in contrast, were found to increase order and balance in the nervous system, and produce smooth, harmonious, sine-wave-like (coherent) heart rhythms. These harmonious rhythms reduce stress and do more: *They actually enhance people's ability to think more clearly and to self-regulate their emotional responses.*[1]

We found that through learning how to decipher the messages we receive from our heart, we gain the keen perception needed to effectively manage our emotions in the midst of life's challenges. The more we learn to listen to and follow our heart intelligence, the more balanced and coherent our emotions become. The more emotionally intelligent people are, the more they have been schooled by the wisdom and intelligence of the heart. Without the regulating influence of the heart's intelligence, our minds easily fall prey to reactive emotions such as insecurity, anger, fear, and blame, as well as other energy-draining reactions and behaviors. It is evident that emotional self-regulation supports access to our heart's intelligence. In addition, mental clarity and intuition are heightened as people learn to shift into a more coherent heart rhythm, which enables them to connect and listen more deeply to their heart's intuitive signals.[12]

Heart Intelligence and Psychology

When I was a student at the University of Chicago studying psychology, I was introduced to cognitive behavioral therapy (CBT), an evolution of psychotherapy designed to help people change their perceptions and thoughts about a situation or event, which in theory would then change their emotional state. CBT is still the most common form of therapy today and many would say the most effective because it's helped millions of people. But, like most methods, CBT works better for some than others. Our deeply held emotional beliefs can undermine our mind's rational and conceptual thinking. A focus on emotional self-awareness and nonjudgmental acceptance of our feelings is often an essential first step in releasing emotional resistance. This opens the heart so that intuitive heart intelligence can provide insight that allows a bigger picture to emerge in our perceptions and facilitate mental and emotional healing.

The ability to manage our emotions, not suppress them but enable them to transform into higher quality feelings and perceptions, is essential for the advancement of individual and collective human consciousness. If we look at history, we see how emotional mismanagement resulting in blame, hate and retribution has created endless loops of suffering on our planet. The power to transform thoughts and emotions into new perceptions is facilitated by learning to listen more deeply to our heart's intuitive guidance and wisdom. This increases the ability to choose our emotional responses instead of mechanically reacting. We can learn to recognize emotions and attitudes that drain us, then replace them with emotions and attitudes that are regenerative and provide more enlightened perspectives. Gaining this ability is one of the primary benefits of practicing tools to access the heart's intelligence.

It can be challenging to distinguish the guidance of our heart from the mental and emotional beliefs that often shape our thoughts. It's encouraging to know that the more we practice discerning the difference between our heart's guidance and our mind's persuasions, it *does* get easier to distinguish them. At the start, it can seem hard and discouraging at times. Yet, with practice, we can learn to recognize that our heart intuition has a different quality or tone than intellectual or conceptual thoughts or emotional desires and beliefs.

You may have found, as I did years ago, that following what you thought was your heart got you into trouble. For example, you might have felt a tingling and your heart beating fast about dating a certain person, but it turned out to be a bad experience. We can easily confuse an emotional sensation for our heart's intuition and follow that allure instead. It takes practice to discern the difference. I learned through trial and error that the lure of attraction isn't always a signal from my true heart.

The heart often whispers to us with quiet common sense. Often it's our heart telling us, "I don't know if I should take the job even though it pays a lot." Then our mind decides to take the job, because in most cases money choices usually win over heart choices until we become empowered by our higher discernment capacities. The mind tends to rationalize our desires and reactions. As my friend Amy says, *When my mind's judgments and reactions are in control, I feel justified in being angry. My heart is decidedly different—softer and simpler. It takes courage to listen to your heart. It might say, 'Just let it go' or 'It's no big deal,' and you may be afraid you're going to let someone get away with something or that the other person is going to walk all over you. But when you have the courage to do what your heart says, you feel better and things seem to work out better.*

To help distinguish between how your head might sound versus your heart, here are some examples:

Driving at Rush Hour. *Head:* Damn this traffic! Stupid driver, slowing everyone down. When are they going to widen this road? She just cut in deliberately! *Heart:* Traffic isn't going to move until it moves—no use getting upset and draining energy. Turn on the radio and listen to some music.

At Work. *Head:* Who does she think she is? It's not fair she gets the good assignments and I'm left with crap—makes me furious! *Heart:* I know things are tough for her and she's running fast. I need to keep my cool, not get sucked into this drama and backbiting. Maybe I'm the one who needs a change in attitude. I think I'll invite her out to lunch.

As you practice listening for the difference in tone, you may find that the mind and heart are like two different radio stations. When you tune to the heart station, your attitude shifts and you look for responses that are better suited for the wholeness of the situation. The mind becomes a big winner in the process. It actually becomes more *rational*. Heart intelligence provides the mind with a bigger picture that allows it to consider what is best for oneself while being more inclusive of the wholeness.

I have also learned that the most effective way to balance my emotional nature and clear unresolved issues is to access my heart and practice self-compassion, compassion for others, appreciation, and kindness. These heart-based practices have increasingly enabled me to distinguish intuitive heart feelings from mental and emotional preferences or concerns. In our research, we found that intuitive insight occurs more frequently when people are aligned with the core values of their heart. Insight often comes as a high-speed intuitive download activated by genuine feelings of appreciation, compassion, or kindness. For example, many people talk about the benefits of appreciation or keeping a gratitude journal. When people express gratitude or appreciation, these are *acts of intelligence* that create more insight and effective outcomes (they are not just something sweet or philosophical).

Many people practice some form of prayer or meditation to discern their heart's intuitive signals. Mindfulness practice has recently become very popular. It teaches people to observe their thoughts and feelings without judging them or getting hooked into them. The practice of "loving kindness" gives you more capacity to do that and is also an important aspect of mindfulness. John Kabat-Zinn, author of numerous books on mindfulness writes: *"Awareness, like a field of compassionate intelligence located within your own heart, takes it all in and serves as a source of peace within the turmoil, much as a mother would be a source of peace, compassion and perspective for a child who was upset. She knows that whatever is troubling her child will pass, so she can provide comfort, reassurance, and peace in her very being. As we cultivate mindfulness in our own hearts, we can direct a similar compassion towards ourselves."* [13]

Humanity will in time come to realize that the heart contains a higher intelligence software package, designed to provide the intuitive guidance needed for navigating life. More people than ever are going to the heart to find greater ease and flow in life. Emotional intelligence is part of it, but people instinctively know there's something seriously intelligent about the heart or they wouldn't say, "When there is nowhere else to go for an answer, go to your heart." The fun question is, why not go there to start with, rather than everywhere else first.

In the coming chapters we will describe more of our research into innate heart intelligence. This research has helped us understand how the heart's intelligence synthesizes other aspects of intelligence to enable us to *become who we truly are.*

NOTES:

1. McCraty, R., Atkinson, M., Tomasino, D., & Bradley, R. T, *The coherent heart: Heart-brain interactions, psychophysiological coherence, and the emergence of system-wide order. Integral Review*, 2009. **5**(2): p. 10-115.

2. Privateer, P.M., *Inventing intelligence: A social history of smart,* 2008: John Wiley & Sons.

3. Weinberg, R.A., *Intelligence and IQ: Landmark issues and great debates. American Psychologist*, 1989. **44**(2): p. 98.

4. Gardner, H., *Frames of Mind, 1985, New York: Basic Books.*

5. Goleman, D., *Emotional Intelligence,* 1995, *New York: Bantam Books.*

6. Fredrickson, B.L., *The role of positive emotions in positive psychology. The broaden-and-build theory of positive emotions. American Psychologist*, 2001. **56**(3): p. 218-226.

7. Lacey, B.C. and J.I. Lacey, *Studies of heart rate and other bodily processes in sensorimotor behavior, in Cardiovascular Psychophysiology: Current Issues in Response Mechanisms, Biofeedback, and Methodology.*, P.A. Obrist, et al., Editors. 1974, Aldine: Chicago. p. 538-564.

8. Lacey, J.I. and B.C. Lacey, *Two-way communication between the heart and the brain: Significance of time within the cardiac cycle. American Psychologist*, 1978(February): p. 99-113.

9. Armour, J.A., *Anatomy and function of the intrathoracic neurons regulating the mammalian heart, in Reflex Control of the Circulation, I.H. Zucker and J.P. Gilmore, Editors.* 1991, CRC Press: Boca Raton. p. 1-37.

10. McCraty, R. and F. Shaffer, *Heart Rate Variability: New Perspectives on Physiological Mechanisms, Assessment of Self-regulatory Capacity, and Health Risk. Glob Adv Health Med*, 2015. **4**(1): p. 46-61.

11. McCraty, R., et al., *The effects of emotions on short-term power spectrum analysis of heart rate variability. Am J Cardiol*, 1995. **76**(14): p. 1089-93.

12. McCraty, R., M. Atkinson, and R.T. Bradley, *Electrophysiological evidence of intuition: Part 2. A system-wide process? J Altern Complement Med*, 2004. **10**(2): p. 325-36.

13. Kabat-Zinn, J. and T.N. Hanh, *Full catastrophe living: Using the wisdom of your body and mind to face stress, pain, and illness,* 2009: Delta.

CHAPTER 4

THE INTUITIVE HEART

By Rollin McCraty

Most of us have been in situations where we felt in our heart the best choice, but instead gave into our mind's fears or desires. Later, we had to backtrack and clear up the problems that resulted. In the last chapter, we described heart intelligence as the "flow of awareness, understanding, and intuitive guidance we experience when the mind and emotions are brought into coherent alignment with the heart."

From my own experience and my observation of others, I realized that the lack of alignment between what our mind says and what our intuitive heart is quietly trying to tell us can be one of the biggest unrecognized sources of stress. It's like being pulled in two different directions. The Greeks viewed these contrasting aspects as being in a constant struggle for control of our inner experience. I've found that intuition doesn't have to be random, fleeting, or in a constant struggle with the mind. With practice, accessing intuition can become integrated into the choices and decisions of our daily lives.

In this chapter, I will provide a brief overview of some of the scientific research that HeartMath and others have done on intuition. Before describing this exciting research, it's helpful to discuss the common ways the term intuition has been defined. The root of the word "intuition" stems from the Latin word *in-tuir*, which can be translated as "looking, regarding, or knowing from within." In most dictionaries, intuition is defined as "the ability to understand or know something, without conscious reasoning." A review of the scientific perspectives on the topic of intuition describe it as "a complex set of interrelated cognitive and bodily processes, in which there is no apparent intrusion of deliberate, rational thought."[1]

Types of Intuition

Historically, most of the research on intuition has focused on the purely cognitive or mental aspects of perception, where intuition is assigned to implicit processes and implicit memory. This type of intuition is a function of the unconscious mind accessing existing information stored away within our brain that we forgot we learned or did not realize we had learned.

It is generally well accepted in scientific circles that there are two separate processing systems used by the brain—this is commonly called dual-process theory. The first is unconscious, automatic, and intuitive. It processes information very rapidly, looking for any similarities between what we are currently seeing or hearing then trying to find a match with past unconscious memories. Therefore, it is relatively undemanding in its use of mental resources.[1] I remember as a child spending time with my grandfather, the town mechanic, and being amazed at his ability to "just listen" to a car or truck idling and often instantly know what the problem was. When someone has gained experience in a particular field, these implicit intuitions are possible because of the brain's capacity to rapidly and unconsciously recognize important cues and match them to familiar ones. In contrast, the second processing system used by our brain is relatively slow and analytical. It's the system where we become conscious of our thoughts about a situation or issue.

Implicit processes can also explain in part what in scientific circles is often called "insight." When we encounter a new problem, one that we cannot quickly solve and may eventually put on the shelf for a while, our brain can still be working on it subconsciously. For instance, when we're in the shower, driving, or doing something else unrelated to the problem, a solution pops into our conscious mind as an intuitive insight—an "aha" or "Eureka" moment. Although implicit processes are an important and common type of intuition, some scientists believe they are the only aspect of intuition. New findings are suggesting this is not the case.

In addition to the implicit memory aspect of intuition, there are two other types of sensitivities that tend to get lumped together under the term intuition, which can make it confusing for people, especially as we talk about a deeper intuition that connects us with the wisdom and guidance from a higher-dimensional aspect of ourselves. All three types of intuition are shown in Figure 1: implicit memory that I described above, along with a second aspect called "energetic sensitivity," and a third called "nonlocal intuition".[2]

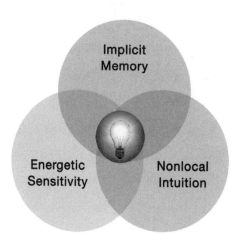

Figure 1 – Three types of sensitivities that the term intuition is used to describe.

Energetic Sensitivity

Energetic sensitivity refers to the ability of our body and nervous system to detect electromagnetic and other types of energetic signals in the environment.[3] This line of research began in our laboratory back in the early 1990s when we were doing research on water. We discovered that water has an unexpected "amplification effect" on weak electromagnetic signals. We also found that different sources of water have slightly different capacities to amplify weak signals. Knowing that the heart radiates a magnetic field which can be detected several feet outside the body with sensitive magnetometers, Mike Atkinson, our laboratory manager, and I came up with the idea to see if we could detect a person's heartbeat in a glass of water.

We placed an electrode in a glass of water and then placed the glass in front of but not touching the person's chest. The experiment worked! Realizing that the human body is 80 percent water, our next step was obvious. We wanted to see if a person's heartbeat could be detected in another person's body and brain. Indeed, we found that we could detect this, which then led to a series of experiments that confirm the electromagnetic signal the heart radiates outwardly into the environment can be detected by other people and animals nearby. Some fun examples were described in Chapter 2 (Josh and his dog, Mabel; Ellen and her horse, Tonopah).

In the next phase of our research we were able to show that information related to our emotional state is encoded in the magnetic field radiated by the heart. In essence, what this means is that a subtle yet influential electromagnetic or "energetic" communication system operates just below our conscious awareness. This communication system energetically connects us to others and helps explain how we can feel or sense another person's presence or emotional state, before receiving any cues from their body language or tone of voice.[3]

Yet another example of this type of intuition involves people who are sensitive to changes in the earth's magnetic fields, many of whom experience more anxiety, increased fatigue, or mental confusion during solar or magnetic storms. In fact, the data from our research suggests that we are all affected to varying degrees by the changing rhythms in the earth's magnetic fields.[4]

Nonlocal Intuition

One of the most frequent comments I have heard over the years from people who have been practicing HeartMath techniques for a while is that their intuition has noticeably increased. They also report experiencing an increased number of synchronicities. The many stories they have told me are clear examples of a type of intuition that could not be explained by past or forgotten knowledge (implicit memory) or by sensing environmental signals (energetic sensitivity). We call this type of intuition "nonlocal intuition" because it transcends the usual limits of time and space. A common story of nonlocal intuition I hear from people, one you may have experienced yourself, is that they spontaneously remember or start thinking about a friend from the past whom they have not talked with or thought about in a long time. Shortly after thinking about that person, the phone rings and sure enough that person is the one calling.

Other common examples of nonlocal intuition are when someone has a clear sense about an event before it occurs, or a mother senses that her child in another part of the world or across town is in distress or has been injured. I have had the privilege to work with a number of law enforcement agencies over the past few years, and when I present our research on nonlocal intuition, there is almost always a story that one of the officers tells about how this type of intuition saved someone's life.

A few years ago when Dean Radin, PhD, the senior scientist at the Institute of Noetic Sciences, was visiting our research lab he told us about the results of a study he had recently conducted which showed that participants' autonomic nervous systems responded before they were shown randomly selected photos that elicited either a negative or a calming emotional response.[5] We immediately saw that his protocol provided a rigorous tool we could use to investigate at least some aspects of nonlocal intuition.

In the following months, we expanded on his experiment by adding additional measures to determine when and where intuitive information about a future event would register in the body and how it would flow through the body, brain, and nervous system. Dr. Radin had focused on using skin conductance levels (SCL), which respond to changes in the sympathetic branch of the nervous system, as his measure of autonomic nervous system activity. In our first study, in addition to skin conductance levels, we included measures of each participant's brain waves (EEG), heart electrical activity (ECG), and heart rate variability (HRV).[6, 7]

In the first of a series of studies, 26 adults who had experience using HeartMath techniques to sustain a heart-coherent state completed the study procedures two different times about two weeks apart. Half of the participants completed the procedures after they had first been in a heart-coherent state for 10 minutes by using a HeartMath technique called Heart Lock-In®, while the other half completed the procedures without doing a Heart Lock-In. The order for both groups was then reversed for the second round of measurements so we could see if being in a coherent state was related to any differences in the results. We suspected this would be likely, as other studies we had conducted found that being in heart coherence before engaging in tasks improved performance and the ability to sustain focus.[8]

The participants thought they were part of a study to test their stress reactions to different types of photographs and were unaware of the study's true purpose. Each was seated in front of a computer screen and instructed to click the mouse when ready to begin each trial. After clicking the mouse, the computer screen remained blank for six seconds. At this point, after all their physiological data had been recorded, a special software program randomly selected the type of photograph to display—one that evoked either a strong emotional reaction or a calm state.

The selected photo was displayed on the screen for three seconds *(see Figure 2 below)*. A blank screen was then shown for an additional 10 seconds, after which a message appeared on the monitor instructing participants to click the mouse again to start the next trial when they were ready. Each participant saw 45 pictures during each of the two times they participated in the experiment. Out of the 45 pictures, 30 were known through previous research to evoke a calm response and 15 pictures were ones known to elicit a strong emotional response.

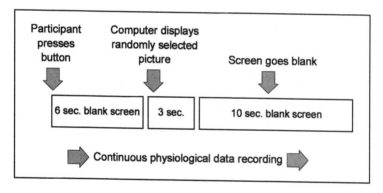

Figure 2 - Experimental setup for the study of nonlocal intuitive perception. Participants viewed a computer monitor and were instructed to press a button when ready to begin each trial. Following the button press, the screen remained blank for six seconds, after which the computer presented a randomly selected image from one of the two picture sets (calm or emotional) and displayed it for three seconds. A blank screen followed for 10 seconds. After this cool-down period, a message appeared on the monitor instructing participants to begin the next trial when ready. Intuitive (pre-stimulus) responses in this study were measured during the six-second blank-screen period *before* the research participant had viewed the randomly selected emotional or calm picture.

The study's results provide some intriguing findings that were published in two research papers as there was too much data to fit into one paper. I will provide some of the highlights here. The study shows that both the heart and the brain appear to be receiving and responding to information about the emotional quality of the picture before the computer had randomly selected it. In other words, the heart and brain appear to be responding to a future event before it happened—in fact 4.8 seconds before the picture was randomly selected by the computer.[6, 7] Keep in mind, the physiological data was collected before the computer had randomly selected the picture that it would display.

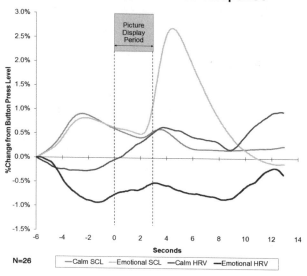

Figure 3 - The heart's pre-stimulus response. The graph shows group averages of the heart rate variability and skin conductance level responses. The "0" time point denotes when the photos were first shown, when participants saw either an emotionally arousing or calm picture. Pre-stimulus responses which indicate nonlocal intuition are in the period between -6 and 0 seconds. The highly significant difference between the HRV responses in the pre-stimulus period before the future calm or emotional photos can clearly be seen starting to diverge approximately 4.8 seconds prior to the participants actually seeing the photos. Surprisingly, there was not a significant difference in the pre-stimulus period for the skin conductance measures.

Even more profound is the data shows the heart receives this information before the brain does. Due to the fact that we had recorded both the brain waves and the electrocardiogram, we were able to do a further analysis called heartbeat-evoked potential analysis. In essence, this allowed us to track the flow or path of the neural signals from the heart to the different regions in the brain. The important finding from this analysis shows that, depending on the emotional quality of the future picture, the heart sends a different pattern of neural signals to the brain before there is a pre-stimulus response anywhere in the brain. Shortly after the signals from the heart arrive at the brain's frontal cortex, a clear pattern of pre-stimulus signals shows up in the brain.

The analysis also found that when participants were in a heart-coherent state before starting the experiment, the signals sent from the heart had a much stronger effect on changing the activity at the frontal areas of the brain. This indicates that when participants were in a more coherent state prior to the experiment, they were more attuned to the intuitive information from the heart.

The results clearly suggest that the heart and brain are connected to a source of information that operates outside the classical boundaries of time and space. In physics this is called nonlocal information. These experiments also suggest that as we practice being in a more heart-coherent state, we have a closer alignment to that source of information.

Further interesting results were obtained in a subsequent study conducted in Iran on nonlocal intuition that used repeat entrepreneurs as the participants. This study applied the same procedures we used in our studies (calm and emotional pictures) but they added an important twist. First they did the experiment with a group of 15 participants who confirmed the results of our original study. Then they did a second experiment with 30 people, but who were in *pairs* and participating in the same procedures at the same time. This was done in order to determine if the nonlocal intuitive effect could be "amplified" by social connection. They found a significantly larger pre-stimulus effect within the pairs of participants than was found in the single participant results. The study authors state that, "...especially changes in the heart rhythm can detect intuitive foreknowledge. This result is notable because it constitutes cross-cultural corroboration. In addition, the results for co-participant pairs offer new evidence on the amplification of the nonlocal intuition signal."[9]

These studies, along with others, have provided compelling evidence that nonlocal intuition can be consistently demonstrated in rigorous experimental conditions by multiple investigators.[10, 11] Furthermore, they have repeatedly demonstrated that the heart's activity appears to be the best[12] physiological indicator of nonlocal information. Somehow, information that is outside of our normal ways of thinking about time and space is available to us. Several scientific theories have been developed in an attempt to better understand how accessing this information is possible, however, no one yet really knows the specific mechanisms.

As mentioned earlier, many perspectives and teachings over the centuries from diverse cultures around the world have spoken of the heart as an access point to the wisdom of our soul or a higher source. Although we cannot say that the nonlocal intuition research described above proves that we have a soul or that there is a universal source of intelligence, it does indicate that the heart is indeed connected to a source of intelligence not bound by the limits of time and space. It just may be that science is on the verge of confirming that the majority of the historical icons of the world's spiritual traditions have been right all along.

Our theory is that there is a connection between the physical heart and the energetic or spiritual heart. And that it provides an access point for intuitive guidance that's much more expansive and inclusive than implicit processes. In our laboratory, we use the term energetic systems to refer to the functions we cannot directly measure, touch, or see, such as our emotions, thoughts, and intuitions. Although these functions have clear correlations with biological activity patterns, they nevertheless remain hidden from direct measurement and observation. Several notable scientists have proposed that such functions operate primarily in the frequency domain (energetic interactions), which by definition, lies outside time and space.[12-15]

In short, our research and personal experience support the hypothesis that the energetic heart has communication channels connecting it with the physical heart, which then communicates intuitive information to the brain's emotional centers and frontal cortex. In Chapter 10, I will discuss how the signals from our heart can modulate our perceptions and emotional experiences.

The practice of building our heart-intuitive connection to our higher capacities is transformational. It enables us to access a source of higher information that streams into our brain and mind via our energetic heart to inform our moment-to-moment perceptions. It provides what we call *practical intuition* where we are more conscious and intuitive at choice points and thus get to choose our actions and reactions rather than mechanically respond in the same old stress-producing behavioral patterns. We see this as the most important function of intuition.

Practical Intuition

Learning how to generate a heart-coherent state to access intuitive intelligence can help prevent many stress-producing scenarios and create a much easier transition and flow through our daily challenges. Practicing heart rhythm coherence a few minutes several times a day helps to attune our mental and emotional nature to the most reasonable and effective way for responding to each situation that life brings us—whether challenging, normal, or creative. Your heart's intuitive guidance is the voice of who you really are.

Here are some practical ways in which practicing heart coherence to access heart intuition can be very helpful:

- Making better choices for higher outcomes

- Increasing your capacity for discerning direction in sensitive situations

- Deciding when it's time to speak up or when it's time to hold back

- Determining what attitude to bring to a particular situation

- Detecting when life is saying a change is needed in attitude, disposition, etc.

- Helping guide diet and health choices

Accessing intuitive guidance is not one quick trick. Some think it is and that's why many people get frustrated with intuition. You have to practice opening and connecting with the heart for intuition to grow within you. Below is the simple Heart Lock-In Technique used in the intuition study to generate a heart-coherent state, which you can practice to build your intuitive connection. Opening your heart, practicing more heart connection with people, and listening from the heart draws in more intuition. Self-compassion, self-forgiveness, and having compassion, forgiveness, and appreciation for others draws in intuition. The heart's intuition includes care for the wholeness of a situation.

Heart Lock-In® Technique

Step 1. Focus your attention in the area of the heart. Imagine your breath is flowing in and out of your heart or chest area, breathing a little slower and deeper than usual.

Step 2. Activate and sustain a regenerative feeling such as appreciation, care, or compassion.

Step 3. Radiate that renewing feeling to yourself and others.

It has been my experience that accessing my intuition takes managing my emotional energy and learning to pay more attention to my heart's promptings. Otherwise, the mind and emotions tend to override the heart's often subtle promptings. As we learn to attune to our heart feelings, our natural intuitive connection can develop and grow. One of the biggest benefits of learning to follow my heart's promptings has been the ability to bring my mental and emotional faculties into greater alignment with my true self.

NOTES:

1. Hodgkinson, G.P., J. Langan-Fox, and E. Sadler-Smith, *Intuition: A fundamental bridging construct in the behavioural sciences. British Journal of Psychology*, 2008. **99**(1): p. 1-27.

2. McCraty, R. and M. Zayas, *Intuitive Intelligence, Self-regulation, and Lifting Consciousness. Glob Adv Health Med*, 2014. **3**(2): p. 56-65.

3. McCraty, R., *The Energetic Heart: Biomagnetic Communication Within and Between People, in Bioelectromagnetic and Subtle Energy Medicine, Second Edition*, P.J. Rosch, Editor 2015.

4. McCraty, R. and A. Deyhle, *The Global Coherence Initiative: Investigating the Dynamic Relationship between People and Earth's Energetic Systems in Bioelectromagnetic and Subtle Energy Medicine, Second Edition*, P.J. Rosch, Editor 2015.

5. Radin, D.I., *Unconscious perception of future emotions: An experiment in presentiment. Journal of Scientific Exploration*, 1997. **11**(2): p. 163-180.

6. McCraty, R., M. Atkinson, and R.T. Bradley, *Electrophysiological evidence of intuition: Part 2. A system-wide process? J Altern Complement Med*, 2004. **10**(2): p. 325-36.

7. McCraty, R., M. Atkinson, and R.T. Bradley, *Electrophysiological evidence of intuition: part 1. The surprising role of the heart. J Altern Complement Med*, 2004. **10**(1): p. 133-43.

8. McCraty, R., Atkinson, M., Tomasino, D., & Bradley, R. T, *The coherent heart: Heart-brain interactions, psychophysiological coherence, and the emergence of system-wide order. Integral Review*, 2009. **5**(2): p. 10-115.

9. Rezaei, S., M. Mirzaei, and M. Reza Zali, *Nonlocal Intuition: Replication and Paired-subjects Enhancement Effects. Global Advances in Health and Medicine*, 2014. **3**(2): p. 5-15.

10. Bem, D.J., *Feeling the future: Experimental evidence for anomalous retroactive influences on cognition and affect*. J Pers Soc Psychol, 2011.

11. Mossbridge, J., P. Tressoldi, E, and J. Utts *Predictive Physiological Anticipation Preceding Seemingly Unpredictable Stimuli: A Meta-Analysis. Frontiers in Psychology*, 2012. **3:390**.

12. Laszlo, E., *Quantum Shift in the Global Brain: how the new scientific reality can change us and our world,* 2008, Rochester, VT: Inner Traditions.

13. Mitchell, E., *Quantum holography: a basis for the interface between mind and matter, in Bioelectromagnetic Medicine*, P.G. Rosch and M.S. Markov, Editors. 2004, Dekker: New York, NY. p. 153-158.

14. Pribram, K.H., *Brain and Perception: Holonomy and Structure in Figural Processing,* 1991, Hillsdale, NJ: Lawrence Erlbaum Associates, Publishers.

15. Tiller, W.A., J. W E Dibble, and M.J. Kohane, *Conscious Acts of Creation: The Emergence of a New Physics,* 2001, Walnut Creek, CA: Pavior Publishing. (pp. 201-202).

CHAPTER 5

RAISING OUR VIBRATION TO ACCESS OUR HIGHER POTENTIALS

By Doc Childre

Each day we process countless *frequencies* through our mind, brain, and heart, such as thoughts, feelings, and emotions. Most of us have heard someone say: "We just can't communicate; we are on totally different frequencies!" or "My brother's vibes (vibrations) seem a little down today," or "The negative vibes were so thick in that room you could trip over them." Many people assume the terms *frequency* and *vibration* (vibes) are only metaphorical expressions; yet many others intuitively realize that our thoughts, feelings, emotions, and intentions are energetic frequencies influenced by beliefs, memories, choices, environmental stimuli, and more. In this writing I'm using terms higher and lower frequency/vibrations to describe the up and down shifts of our moods, attitudes, behaviors, disposition, etc. Sometimes we operate in a higher vibration and sometimes a lower one. It varies throughout the day, week, or month, depending on how well we manage our energy in response to our interactions with life, others, or within ourselves.

When our vibrations are up, our heart energy flows through our interactions. We naturally generate uplifting feelings from a more empowered demeanor. We are kinder, more gracious and we *genuinely* connect with others. We respond to stressful situations with soundness and clearer discernment. We are less vulnerable to frustration, impatience, anger, or anxiety, and we feel more self-secure and less critical of others. We are drawn to notice nature, flowers, and trees that we usually sleep-walk past, as our preoccupations rob us of this gift of conscious connection.

When our vibrations are down, we can experience separation from others due to judgments or blame, excessive worry, and low self-security, along with empty care for others because of being too preoccupied with our self and our story. We are quicker to become angry, impatient, frustrated—the list.

At times radical frequency shifts in our moods and perceptions cause us to feel like we are two different people in the same body. Our behaviors and responses can become significantly different depending on the frequency of our disposition—higher, lower, or bouncing in-between. In our higher vibration we don't have to *try* to be positive, because uplifting feelings and thoughts automatically flow through our system. Our heart energy is more present which increases our authentic connection with others. In a lower vibration we tend to allow negative thoughts and feelings the license to roam and feed from our life force. As we *feed lower thoughts*, they are inclined to *run our life*.

The good news is that we are not predestined victims of random frequency modulations. Through the day we can learn to consciously intervene, *reset*, and lift our attitudinal vibration to handle whatever comes up more cost-effectively. That's the long way of saying that *we have choice*—and connecting with our heart's intuitive choices is the new frontier.

How Living in a Lower Vibration Affects Our Well-Being

More people are finding it harder to breathe out and relax through a day without looking over their shoulder to see if everything is okay. That was one of my main challenges. For a long time I ran constant anxiety and even when life seemed great I couldn't be at peace or feel that everything was okay. I thought a steady current of anxiety was normal and didn't bear any consequences, until my health started telling a different story. This led to a wake-up call and the realization it was my ego vanity that was creating performance anxiety and glitchy peace. With my heart's support, I did a reset and started appreciating the good in my life, rather than living in suspicion of what was not.

Continuous low-grade anxiety can generate a streaming energy deficit, even if we are unconscious of it. Many of us have been trapped in this lower vibration and paid the price time and time again. Operating in a lower vibration has a numbing effect and we fail to see the red flag drop. It becomes our *perception of reality*, and we forget that we *can change* how we respond to the scenes of our life. We can't prevent all unpleasant situations that come our way, but we are responsible for how we handle them. Yet, we get so acclimatized to lower emotional habits that they feel permissible and *not accountable*. These cumulative stress deficits *are* accountable and become catalysts for accelerated aging, health issues, and spiritual dismay.

External stressors, such as financial and survival pressures, health problems, work-related challenges, relationship problems—these are some of the standard triggers that lure our thoughts and feelings into a lower vibration and ramp up the stress. How can we not feel this way at times? I'll discuss how we can progressively manage these stressors, but let's first look at what they can cause.

When our vibes are low, our feelings become lackluster as does our connection with others. There are more mistakes and do-overs; we tend to make shortsighted choices in our personal and business life, along with experiencing low to high anxiety which fuels insecurities. This can eventuate into different degrees of depression, brain fog, and fading confidence. It's happening to millions of people. We're not bad for experiencing this, but that doesn't make our energy deficits disappear.

When we don't know how to raise the vibration of our disposition, we can stay trapped for days or months in predictable stress-producing patterns that become our norm. Being stuck in these patterns withers our quality of life while keeping us hamster-hiking on the same old "dread-mill"—and blaming others because it squeaks.

Our thoughts and feelings influence the chemistry that regulates much of our health—how we feel, for better or worse. With meaningful intention, we *can* begin to turn these energy deficits around as we realize that our thoughts, feelings, emotions, and attitudes are just *frequencies* that can be changed—once we put our heart into our intention. From kids through adulthood, we've been told to "put your heart into it" when pursuing matters important to us. This is because at subjective levels we instinctively know that the power of our heart's commitment can often defy odds and triumph in seemingly unachievable situations. It's time to bring our heart online.

Heart Qualities for Self-Transformation

We often hear that we only use a small percent of our brain. Wait until science realizes what a small percentage of our heart's potential we utilize. One of the aims of HeartMath research is to help verify this, along with facilitating easier ways to access the endless benefits of our heart's intelligent guidance. The good news is that we don't have to wait for the blessing of science before we can draw unlimited benefits from our intuitive heart's guidance.

Old, unwanted habit patterns change more gracefully as our heart and mind partner in supporting our commitments. For most of us, deeper emotional imprints from the past are harder to change. Some of our challenges need to be addressed a little at a time, in segments. Stuck emotional patterns can be similar to rusted bolts that require being soaked in solvent to dissolve the resistance. As we learn to acknowledge and accept our difficulties and resistances gracefully, it acts as a powerful solvent that frees up our heart's resilience and guidance for handling life's challenges more effectively.

Significance

Making peace with our resistances gets easier as we learn that much of our lack of peace comes from the *unmanaged significance* we assign to issues. For example: It's increased significance that turns a simple concern into obsessive worry or turns a little anxiety into pressing fear. Unbridled significance over-swells the size of our challenges, especially emotional challenges. Excessive significance and drama create doubt in our capacity to cope, which sparks low-grade and high-intensity anxiety.

The upside is we can learn to consciously reduce the significance we feed lower thoughts and feelings to stop this piracy of our personal vitality and peace. Practicing acceptance and self-compassion (not self-pity) creates a soaking effect that reduces the emotional significance which blocks clear assessment for better options. As we reduce significance, we are quickly rewarded because we start to see clearer perceptions of what our highest choices and directions would be.

We often make high-spirited commitments for behavior changes and then get stuck from not having the patience, self-acceptance, and self-compassion needed to support our process of change. We forget to use these heart qualities right at the time they would benefit us most. Don't feel awkward about giving yourself self-acceptance and compassion without being self-critical, though most people have a hard time with that. Simply think of it as giving yourself some latitude. Self-acceptance and self-compassion are important, but they are just a start in managing and reducing stressful challenges. Throughout this book we provide effective approaches and tools to help us go deeper in addressing and transforming these complex issues. Let's now explore key ways to prevent some of our main stress accumulators.

Rushed Energy

Rushed, impatient energy diffuses our capacity for favorable outcomes when we're involved in sensitive discernments regarding choices. When we push energy, this cancels the experience of ease and creates hiccups in our intentions. Patience and ease actually create the energetic environment for coherent flow to take place in our communications, choices, and actions. It's our mind that tends to rush energy; our heart chooses balance, rhythm, and flow. When cooperating together they increase outcomes that fit the need of the situation.

Rhythm has to do with the timing and sensitivity in our actions. (It's similar to the way physical rhythm helps minimize the clunks in our dance steps.) In high school I remember pushing energy trying to learn complex dance steps in the Irish jig, and the more I pushed the more I was fussed at by my teacher. The more I was fussed at, the harder I pushed, and the more I clunked until I was put on the second-string dance team. The teacher explained that I was pushing so hard from the mind to learn the steps that it blocked me from learning a most important part—the rhythm.

As I grew up, I saw this play out in many life situations where people trip over themselves from pushing energy against flow (like swimming upstream). The magic from applying balance, rhythm, and flow is that it prevents and dissolves stress and resistances while on the move.

Learning how to do this becomes *an advantage leap* once we understand the importance of internal energy economy.

Shifting Lower-Attitude Frequencies

We're all aware that certain attitudes or tendencies can be tougher to shift. But the process becomes easier once our mind agrees to cooperate more harmoniously with our heart's intuitive feelings. More people are intuitively sensing that they have the capacity to re-write depleting emotional behavioral patterns. When our mind's perception aligns with our heart's intuitive assessment, a bigger picture comes into view and new possibilities and solutions emerge.

Attitudes and perceptions are like pre-set frequencies that we store and activate at times, depending on how we feel or if we are in a higher or lower vibration. Most all of us have practiced maintaining an uplifting attitude as this allows more access to the "flow" in our interactions. Often, when we are challenged by a decision, someone tells us, "Relax, you have choices." However, when we are operating in our lower-frequency attitude, we filter out our most *effective choices* and perceptions. We tend to only see *inferior choices* and we go with them, time and time again repeating the same lessons unlearned. We often have to repeat our lessons before we attain the take-home value. When tired of learning the same lessons, we can connect with our heart and take responsibility, bypass the drama and blame, and move forward with what we've learned. Sometimes this flows smoothly, and sometimes the moving parts grind a little through the transition.

Negative Thoughts and Feelings

At times random negative thoughts stream through us all. Many of these thoughts and feelings can pass quickly if we reduce the drama and significance we assign to them. We are not bad for having negative thoughts, but we can refuse to become a yo-yo-bot of their stressful creations. There are many energy leaks that lower our vibration and performance, such as irritation, impatience, frustration, etc. These *assumed* small energy leaks, for example impatience, often turn into blockbuster energy deficits over time if we don't reset and transform them into a higher vibration—like patience, resilience, and latitude. Low-vibrational habits restrict our flow of spirit, which eventually creates glitches in our major operating systems—mental, emotional, physical (nervous system and more). This increases our vulnerability to the standard health problems experienced from constant overload in our emotional system.

As we genuinely desire it, our *heart's intuitive prompter* will begin to signal us when our vibration is low and we are spiraling into a stress deficit from energy drain. The signal from our heart's intuitive prompter becomes clearer as we listen to it. It alerts us when we are seduced back into old patterns that are not who we choose to be and also supports us in re-firing our healthy commitments and attitudes. Most of us are connected with our heart's prompter to some degree (it's often called conscience). This connection progressively opens the door for receiving our inner guidance. Some of us know from experience that intuition is more likely to jam up when approached from a desperate mind—but is more accessible in the stillness of a calm and open heart.

Quick Exercise for Replacing Lower-Vibrational Feelings

The following short and simple exercise can be helpful in replacing lower-vibrational feelings. (It's similar to the "Overcare Exercise" provided in a later chapter.)

1. Pick a time when you feel sad or insecure, disconnected from others, or any lower-vibrational feelings or attitudes you would want to replace and feel better.

2. Find a place to breathe quietly for a few minutes and with each breath imagine your mind, emotions, and body getting still inside.

3. From that place of stillness, imagine the kind of caring feeling or attitude you would like to have, or have felt before when you were more self-secure. As you breathe, imagine that you are breathing this new feeling into your being.

4. The last step is to breathe this feeling and attitude for a few minutes to anchor it in. Try it again later if it doesn't work. Sometimes we give up too quickly on the things that would benefit us the most.

With a little practice, you can surprise yourself with increased inspiration and heart power to change many unwanted feelings, emotions, and attitudes that reduce your resilience and ability to feel good. And, when you are feeling uplifting feelings and attitudes such as gratitude, kindness, or compassion, do this exercise to anchor in these feelings so they will return more often.

It's helpful to remember that small children often use their imagination to *quickly* transform their feelings from anger and frustration into elation and happiness. We each have this capacity as adults too, but we accumulate so many handed-down mind-driven programs, that it creates a decline in the direct heart connection and emotional resilience we had as kids. As adults we usually have to practice with commitment to reawaken this direct connection to our heart's energy, and then integrate it into our interactions. This creates more balanced decisions and a straighter path to our best outcomes.

Practice shifting small unwanted feelings and eventually you'll find yourself replacing stronger unwanted feelings, habits, and mindsets. The door to the hidden power of our heart can be opened, but sometimes we have to jiggle the handle a few times to loosen up the resistance.

More Tips to Raise Your Frequency Pitch (Vibration)

Reconnecting with heart feelings throughout the day, such as gratitude, kindness, compassion, patience, and flow, keeps our vibration up while preventing and eliminating many merry-go-round energy deficits. These heart qualities serve to facilitate our overall health and well-being.

Another effective way to raise our vibration is to take a few days and appreciate connections and friendships that we have adapted to or unintentionally taken for granted. *Adapting* creeps into our relationships in a stealthy, hard-to-recognize, fashion. Then it quietly reduces the warmth and the "zing" in our connections. Take a heart stand not to let caring relationships wilt from adapting! As we make appreciation and gratitude *a way of life*, this offsets adapting and keeps the spirit within our connections alive and self-replenishing. Gratitude and kindness are two of *love's* most magnetic expressions which draw to us the highest best that life has to offer.

The higher vibration of our true self naturally generates the textures of kindness and respect and other qualities which are core heart frequencies that harmonize our life's exchanges. Heart textures such as gratitude and compassion naturally radiate from us when our heart is engaged in our connections and communications. Humanity is evolving past *pilot-light care* (low heart warmth), which only produces surface level interactions that are missing the regenerative benefits of authentic connection.

In general, our hearts are warmer to our family, pets, and our circle of friends. As we spiritually mature, our heart warmth expands to include more people in its care, and our respect for nature increases. We desire to be part of something that makes a difference—something that serves the greater whole of humanity. From there our love matures into unconditional love, without borders. In this higher vibration we are more directly connected with our heart's guidance for creating joy and fulfillment while supporting others to do the same.

Many books and articles have been written on the efficacy of practicing the core qualities of the heart. These primary attributes not only raise our personal vibration, they help to lift the environmental vibration as well. We spiritually prosper each time we refresh these natural transformative heart qualities. Don't think of your practice as a discipline; see it as a free pass to your own high-end health spa with beneficial results.

The Active Ingredients in Prayer and Meditation

One of the major subjective values of *heart-connected* prayers or meditations is that they often leave us with a feeling of warmth and confirmation. More and more people are exploring a deeper connection with their heart because it doesn't take away or compete with their religion, spiritual path, or basic belief system. It strengthens it.

Being genuine and heart-connected with your feelings provide the activating ingredients in prayer, meditation, etc. We all have felt the obvious difference between genuine appreciation and counterfeit appreciation. When appreciation is not genuine, it's not real—it's no more effective than a "store mannequin" trying to appreciate window shoppers. For instance, when blessing our food, we know the difference when we are heart-connected or when we are mechanically repeating a memorized prayer (while worrying if we are going to get a homemade biscuit because half of the soccer team suddenly showed up hungry, unannounced). When prayers and meditations run split screens with other preoccupations, they won't raise our vibration and we usually end up with wasted time filled with unfocused mind traffic.

Inner Stillness

Many spiritual cultures agree that *inner stillness* creates an energetic environment for supporting our advancing consciousness which can unleash the transformational power of our love. That's why from the beginning of HeartMath, many of the tools and especially the coherence technology have been designed to facilitate easier access to stillness and its connection to our natural inner wisdom and guidance. Think of inner stillness as a practical asset for deeper listening. How many times have we told children or others to *get still inside* and listen up, because we have something important to tell them? This is because we instinctively know that inner stillness plays a part in the quality and depth of most people's hearing ability. So why not use it the way it can count the most— to quiet our own mental and emotional static so that we can hear the counsel and wisdom from our heart's intuitive guidance.

When our mind quietens, inner stillness is where we land. From there we can reset and upgrade our life's experience. We often hear ourselves and others say, "If I had more *foresight*, I would have handled that situation differently." Stillness is a primary source for increasing our foresight and discernment. Inner stillness is a place where our heart can speak without the mind running it off the road. In order to "be still, and know" we first have to be still enough to listen.

It's highly effective to schedule times for practice of inner stillness to allow our heart, mind, and emotions to experience a relaxed time-out from competing over the choices we make. Stillness softens our determined mental and emotional traffic so that our heart-speak can be heard. This requires practice because the mind will try to occupy any available space if the door is left cracked. However, if stillness practices didn't produce high-value results, think of all the centuries of time that meditators and spiritually conscious people would have wasted throughout history. With fine-tuning, inner stillness becomes like a personal elevator to our highest view and eliminates the weariness from climbing endless stairs. I feel that practicing inner stillness will become a most positive corner-turning step forward for humanity, not as a trend or religious motivation but as a street-sense way of life. You can try this inner stillness exercise that I found valuable for deepening my connection to my heart's intelligent guidance.

Inner Stillness Exercise:

Step 1: As you breathe quietly, imagine your breath calmly slowing down the vibration of your mental and emotional energy. Stay with it and don't care if your mind disrupts you. This will improve with patience and practice.

To get benefits out of this stillness exercise, you don't have to totally stop the mind—even reducing thoughts and calming yourself improves your capacity to sense your heart feelings and suggestions. In a short amount of time, the power to quieten your mind will increase.

Step 2: As you feel your energy calming, genuinely radiate love to something or someone you care about. This connects you with your heart energy.

Step 3: While maintaining your state of calmness, ask your heart for guidance, solutions, or deeper understanding regarding life issues you are experiencing.

Step 4: Imagine stillness as a peaceful place where you are taking a time-out. As thoughts come up, don't push against them. Casually refocus on breathing love and peace into the stillness. Our higher choices become more obvious as we increase our capacity to listen in stillness to our heart's intelligent guidance.

Note: When you're listening for intuition, don't expect a Siri or an Alexa-type attendant on the other end with a download of answers. Especially on complex issues, intuitive feeling answers often come later—through something someone says, something you read, while you're in the shower, driving down the road, etc.

So how can we take the benefits from inner stillness exercises, meditations, or prayers into our day-to-day activities? Operating from a *state of ease* is a natural practice for bringing the essence of stillness into our daily interactive mode. We can learn to do this by breathing the attitude of *ease* at times throughout the day. Breathing the attitude of ease helps us to step down the carry-over effects of our inner stillness practices into our normal interactions and activities.

When we discern our direction from a place of inner ease, this helps prevent the impatience of our mind from overriding the intuitive feelings of our higher choices. Acting from a place of inner ease is a heart-intelligent skill in the economy of personal energy management. The state of inner ease reduces many decision-making regrets and also helps to access the magic of flow in our processes. Flow provides the straightest line to manifesting our intentions. *(Moving in the state of ease is discussed thoroughly in the next chapter.)*

Intuitive Connection

Connecting with our heart's intuition (inner guidance) can advance our capacity to take charge of our life's decisions and direction. Our spiritual heart is a most beneficial, yet under-used aspect of our true nature and potential. When our mind is not aligned with our heart, it often favors our lower-vibrational choices in decisions, more than supporting the highest outcomes for all concerned. This pattern accumulates an energy deficit that feeds back in our physical and emotional system. Then our vibration drops and we target something to blame.

A helpful way to encourage intuitive connection is to soften our posture on *knowing what we know* too quickly about everything. As my self-awareness increased, I realized that I was crafty at blocking my intuition so it wouldn't compete with having "made up my mind" about what I wanted. Then I realized most of humanity is also good at that, which is one of the biggest reasons that heart intuition hasn't made its way into the mainstream as a most intelligent, personal guidance system. It's humorous how often people *reject their heart's intuitive feelings* and go with their ego choices—and then take meditation classes *hoping to develop intuitive guidance*. I'm sure many of us have experienced that along the way.

Our intuitive heart can foresee our higher outcome options and offer our mind and emotions better choices for navigating life's situations. Deep heart listening in stillness can create the energetic link to the wisdom and directions from our true self (soul, higher self, source, or whatever you want to call it based on your cultural beliefs, spiritual beliefs, or experiences). Fussing over getting the "right name" is not as important in the process of moving forward spiritually as one might think. For convenience, I often bundle them all together and refer to them as *"my large, or my higher potential."* For example, if a resistance comes up in my life, I simply get still in my heart and connect with *my large* for effective suggestions.

In times past, I searched unceasingly for the magic of intuitive access, the glamorous aspects—psychic abilities, seeing the future, lottery numbers, etc., rather than looking for inner guidance, deeper discernment, and grounded choices. It's normal to desire that which coddles the ego when we first get enamored with intuition and its possibilities. Later, stress from health problems influenced me to explore intuition more for insights regarding my day-to-day choices and ways to serve humanity. As we put first things first, then the extras can naturally unfold as add-ons to our fulfillment, but not be a driving force that decides our fulfillment.

With that said, I still could enjoy winning a mega-million-dollar lottery and heading straight to the local "Dollar Store" to do some serious binge shopping without having to even glance at the price tags! *(Humor)* We don't have to prove that we're frugal and feel apologetic if our personal abundance includes finer things. Many people know this at the conceptual level, but for some, their emotions are still trapped in shades of guilt—causing them to experience wealth through a restricted state of enjoyment. If you are experiencing this, it's time to lose those restrictions and quit punishing your joy.

Our Inner Dignity

True dignity, not pretended, is a powerful heart frequency that supports the maintenance of inner composure, especially when the tone of our integrity starts to weaken. At times we can feel exhausted and insecure from the weight of change, and that's understandable. This is a perfect opportunity to renew our dignity and practice self-compassion to replenish our resilience—especially when life presses us with choices faster than our capacity to sort out our moves. When holding the vibration of dignity and poise, we are more effective at preventing and reducing incessant worrying (hurried aging).

Our inner dignity is one of the primary motivators for self-empowered actions. Dignity lifts us to realms of new possibilities where things begin to transform, creating more stability in our lives. Undesirable patterns begin to disappear, and new patterns emerge as a new way of life. Our dignity is the foundational baseline of good character. It's a source of extra strength we can draw upon, especially at times when we are low on initiative. Here's an exercise to connect with your inner dignity.

Inner Dignity Exercise:

1. Focus your attention in the area of the heart. Imagine your breath is flowing in and out of your heart or chest area, breathing a little slower and deeper than usual. Find an easy rhythm that's comfortable.

2. Imagine you are consciously increasing your inner dignity, inner strength, and poise as you breathe. Do this for a few minutes, with feeling. This increases your power to maintain your higher principles through day-to-day interactions.

3. Explore how increasing your inner dignity can encourage you to follow through on choices that are best for you, even though they are not always

the most appealing. Dignity provides a strength that keeps us aligned with our higher principles. It strengthens with use.

At the core level we are caring beings, regardless of the veneer and cloaking behaviors we've picked up along the way. The collective heart awakening on the planet is nudging us to remove our disguises and start showing up more as who we are.

True Self

Our true self represents an achievable vibration within us that contains the wisdom and intelligence of our heart. In this higher vibration, we are harmoniously connected with the hearts of others and all life. We naturally exude unconditional love and compassion that's not diluted from over-attachment to others, issues, or outcomes. Our spiritual advancement is not furthered by trying to be perfect. Accepting our fallibility is a leap towards becoming authentic. Increased authenticity unfolds as we raise the vibration of our spirit with heartfelt connections, nonjudgment, and acceptance, while including ourselves in our love.

Operating continuously in the higher vibration of our true self is not expected of us overnight. It's a process that unfolds at the rate-of-genuine commitment—if we don't waste our spunk peeping over our shoulder to gloat at our progress. When we overanalyze progress we risk stopping it in its tracks, especially if it's used just for ego inflation. Increasingly, more of us now desire to reset our life with a fresh start by leading with the heart and preceding with love in areas that we normally keep roped off. We have our reasons for keeping our heart at arm's length from others, but maybe it's time to challenge these reasons to see if they are handed-down behaviors that don't represent who we really are.

Humanity is transitioning into a state of consciousness that will unleash the creative power of togetherness, and the understanding that it's our heart vibration that qualifies the difference between separation and feeling connected. Increased heart-connected interactions will progressively raise the vibration of collective conscious-ness. This will set the stage for realizing that inclusive, unconditional love and compassion is the next advanced mode of intelligent living. Millions of people, and consis-tently more, will be benefiting from this new awareness long before the whole of humanity chooses it. Individual choices and timing have to be allowed without judgment and condescension. As more of us practice operating from our true self, the restorative power of our collective compassion naturally increases. This will make it easier for others to free themselves from limited beliefs that repress the human potentials which reside in the hidden power of the heart. The door to the global heart is opening and I suggest that love will increasingly pour its way through the streets.

CHAPTER 6

MOVING IN A STATE OF EASE

By Doc Childre

"Ease" is an inner state that helps us transit more smoothly through the energies and rhythms of our life's experiences. Operating in the state of inner ease increases our sensitive connection with our heart's intuitive guidance to provide practical solutions or effective options for responding to most situations.

Many people conceptually understand the value of ease, but our pressing minds and emotions tend to override the wisdom to actually practice it—especially when deeper discernment and wiser choices are needed. As the speed of life keeps accelerating, the mind and emotions can become overstretched from having to make decisions too quickly due to overload from high-pressured responsibilities. Even what people call the "Now" seems to have sped up—it used to last a full moment but I think that extra time is shrinking.

The practice of operating from the state of ease helps to slow down the vibratory rate of the mind and emotions so our heart's intuitive feelings can weigh in on choices and actions. In most cases, the speed and aggression of the mind and emotions drown out our heart's directions for more effective outcomes. The state of inner ease doesn't bog down our thinking; it clears it up.

Several HeartMath research studies have confirmed the benefits of practicing ease. In these studies, breathing ease played a pivotal role in helping participants slow the vibration of their mind and emotions so that their heart's intuitive feelings could be translated into higher reasoning and choices.

Let's take a deeper look at a few of the ways that people already naturally use ease in daily life, along with some advanced ways to use ease for achieving desired outcomes. This will help to broaden our understanding and respect for the benefits and advantages of this common-sense practice.

Moving with ease includes an aspect of stillness. It's an active stillness, rather than the stillness we try to attain in meditation. When people ease the vibration of the mind and emotions in conversation, they listen smarter, they hear deeper, their comprehension increases, and we feel heard—which is a rare treat nowadays. (The humor is that we can feel the benefits and intelligence of ease when others are listening from that place, yet we can go a year and not think about easing up in our interactions.)

It's important to note that ease is not a floaty-blissy or sleepy-headed state. I know the term ease sounds soft, like a butterfly practicing ballet or such, but don't underestimate its power or effectiveness.

Highly trained athletes can run races while maintaining a state of ease in their mind and emotions. Olympic athletes especially know that when their mind and emotions are at ease and in check, it enables a resonant alignment between heart, mind, and emotions which bolsters their power to achieve their aim. This results in higher scores and outcomes. Also, when we are in a state of ease our emotions rebound quicker if disappointments or setbacks occur, which is important.

Navy SEALs and other special forces units utilize HeartMath's coherence technology for increasing personal coherence which helps sustain a state of inner ease. This practice increases alertness and receptivity to intuitive input when discerning critical situations and choices.

People tell each other at times to "ease up and find the flow." An advanced practice for finding the flow is learning to create the flow, especially in nonflowing situations. We have the power in our heart to do this. When a seasoned surfer experiences the flow, it's not dependent on having perfect waves—flow is especially about how gracefully she adjusts to daunting waves or turbulent weather. She is poised in inner balance and creates her own rhythm and flow to suit each environmental circumstance.

We all are constantly surfing through life's potentials along with its challenges and inconsistencies. How we greet them decides our ratio of flow and capacity to adapt. Inner ease generates flow by helping to regulate the balance and cooperation between our heart, mind, and emotions (coherence).

Each day people are telling each other to "just breathe." What we're saying is yes, breathe, but add an intentional attitude of calm and ease as you breathe. As you consciously breathe, casually imagine breathing in an attitude of calm and ease.

It's important to learn to feel if you really are in ease instead of assuming it. Remembering to breathe ease throughout the day will help anchor the pattern into your cellular memory, which shortens the time for the practice to become automatic. You'll see benefits soon when this practice is genuine.

Here are some examples of times to breathe ease for a while:

- When you want to prevent or reduce anxiety.

- When you get caught in a drama-fest type of situation. (Breathing ease helps you remember that if you can't leave the situation, you can practice being "in" it, but not "of" it.)

- To prevent or restore energetic composure from overwhelm.

- Before and during meetings. (Breathing the attitude of ease sets an internal environment for deeper listening, better comprehension, and staying emotionally poised. However, if your composure crashes, breathing ease helps you re-center quicker, especially if you are caught in a heated dispute.)

- Before you respond to a vexing email, breathe ease to settle the mind and emotions. (You often can prevent an emotional mess, not to mention the energy spent and downtime it takes for damage control.)

- To access or restore patience and resilience whenever needed. (Ease is usually the missing ingredient when we are impatient. Breathing ease creates the tolerance that disarms impatience.)

- While discerning important issues or choices. (To slow down your mental and emotional traffic so that intuitive insight can be perceived.)

- When you want to be creative, as ease draws (or unleashes) intuitive direction.

- Before sleep if you have sleep problems.

- When life's challenges are coming in faster than solutions.

With each breath, simply draw in the feeling of inner ease to balance your mental and emotional energy. Set a meaningful intent to anchor the feeling of casual ease as you engage in projects, challenges, or daily activities.

The Power of Pause

We would be alarmed by how much extra stress we accumulate from decisions that we could have handled more skillfully—if we had *eased* into our reasoning processes and taken *pause*.

We've all had moments when we thought to *pause*— to allow ourselves the chance to regain clarity and calm, and tune into what would be an intelligent response in the next moment. Yet, even knowing the value of pausing, we can still create stress overload if we allow time pressures or frustrations to block our intuition prompting us to: *pause before engaging*. Emails that we wish we could take back serve as obvious examples, among many others. Learning the power of *pause* can prevent some of our largest stress deficits, especially in times of change and uncertainty.

Also, practicing inner ease and pause during times of increased electromagnetic or solar activity and planetary changes can save a lot of energy, angst, and downtime. These environmental influences often trigger increased excitability, which may affect our mental/emotional behavioral patterns in unexpected ways (memory lapses, brain fog, anxiety, fear, edginess, aches in odd places, sleeplessness, elation, depression, and more). When you experience these symptoms, it's helpful to breathe ease and take deeper pause for discerning and double-checking communications and decisions. Take life a segment at a time and practice discerning your steps from a state of ease.

For many of us, knowing how to pause and access inner ease is not the problem—it's *remembering* to do it, especially when it counts the most. This gives us a chance to act and respond from our real self rather than from our mechanical "predictable other." Ease is a higher-vibrational gift from the intelligence of the heart.

CHAPTER 7

BECOMING OUR TRUE SELF
AND
FINDING OUR PURPOSE

By Doc Childre

Many people want to increase their care, compassion and other expressions of love, though they are not involved in any particular belief system. There are countless beliefs and theories regarding source, higher self, soul, etc. If such terms don't resonate with your perceptions and beliefs, you can disregard them because it won't hinder your progress along the path to becoming who you truly are. Your own spirit will bring you an increasing understanding of your true self and the path to unfold your higher potentials in perfect timing. Nowadays it's important for individuals to increasingly rely on their own heart's evaluations, especially with the flood of new information emerging which explores spirituality, consciousness, inner and outer space, and such. We can all expect that our perceptions and beliefs will refine along the way as our awareness expands. That's normal; it's part of forward movement.

To me the most important thing to turn the tide of global stress is increasing our care, compassion, and cooperation with each other. I feel we are way moving forward on the spiritual path if we open our hearts and serve each other through love and compassionate care. Increasing love and care for others and discerning day-to-day guidance from my heart's intuitive feelings has brought me more in touch with the true sense of who I am. If I make mistakes along the way, I make a heartfelt commitment to make adjustments.

Living more from the heart creates resonance between our heart, mind, brain, and emotions. When these powerful energies are not resonating as a team, and have opposing desires and agendas, this generates much (or most) of our stress accumulation. These divisions cause incoherence, which represses the spirit and heart energy that supply our joy, well-being, and access to our heart's intuition. When our heart energy is low, we feel less care and connection with others and more scattered within ourselves. Our attempts at happiness are often half-baked and vulnerable to constant disruption. We can change this as we realign our mind and emotions with our heart a few times throughout the day. Practicing heart coherence is important for boosting intuitive connection, resilience, and emotional balance, especially during times of personal or global stress. Our spirit supports us in becoming more coherent, as this is the optimum frequency and vibration for creating harmony, better choices, and fulfillment. Coherence between our heart, mind, and emotions is also the baseline for wholeness healing practices.

My perception is that humanity's collective purpose is to raise the vibration of consciousness to connect with the heart's intelligent guidance. Our heart's wisdom is there to facilitate us with unconditional love, healing, and intelligent direction. This creates an energy field that supports a harmonious foundation for creating peace and a planet that thrives, not just survives. For ages it's been said that within our hearts our questions can be answered, along with guidance and directions for fulfillment. I suggest that this will become more accepted and increasingly validated by many individuals in the foreseeable future. More people are feeling increased curiosity regarding their true self, along with deeper listening to their heart's feelings and suggestions.

When exploring our spiritual heart's potentials in prayer or meditation, we progressively learn to distinguish the difference between our heart's guidance and our mind's foolery. Most of us have felt the swinging-door of unsureness when discerning our inner voice; we may occasionally even wonder if our prayers and meditations ever land on anyone's desk up there that matters.

Discerning our heart's directions and choices will refine as the sensitivity to our higher-vibrational feelings increases, which it will with genuine commitment. Casually imagine the heart's voice as an integral part of your true self, like a buddy that offers a handy, helicopter-view of less cluttered pathways and directions through life's opportunities or challenges. Having a genuine heart's desire to connect with your higher guidance helps to draw its facilitation. We still have to make choices, yet our higher choices become more obvious as we increase our capacity to listen in stillness to the heart's intelligent guidance. Our heart steps down higher-vibrational choices from our true self and nudges us in the direction of our highest purpose. Don't feel that you are unworthy of your higher facilitation and guidance. Becoming your best involves merging with this higher aspect of who you truly are.

Following our heart's guidance expands our awareness to be more inclusive of the whole of humanity, as we realize we are all energetically connected. Deepening our care for each other creates easier access to our true self's assistance. Our true self is not perched in a castle at the top of countless flights of stairs. Many of us have already climbed those stairs, and now it's time to cease the heavy lifting and find a straighter line to our higher potentials. One simple way we can support an increased connection with our higher capacities is to learn to quietly breathe our way into the stillness of our heart space to connect more with our true self.

Here's a way this works for me. I sit quietly for a few minutes and breathe consciously. On the in-breath, I imagine breathing in divine love throughout my being. On the out-breath, I radiate the feeling of gratitude. Doing this lifts the vibration of my spirit and helps to bring my heart, mind, and emotions into coherent alignment and stillness. This resonance creates an energetic conduit for the care and guidance from my true self to integrate more easily into my day-to-day human interactions. If you decide to try this, be patient while getting the feel of the process. Without patience, your mind will tend to expect too much too quickly and you will likely give up, disappointed.

Our true self, through intuition, suggests the most effective ways to facilitate us based on our highest needs, which is not always what our personality requests (though often it is). In our present time, we are creating the blueprint for our future with our thoughts and feelings regarding self and others. As we progressively merge with our true self, this serves to magnetize a more fulfilling life and increased peace. We become more capable of manifesting our full potential. We serve others and expand our love past our small circle to include the greater collective. People are already experiencing this, especially many in the younger generation. They have their share of challenges, but seem more connected with their natural abilities, talents, and gifts from their higher potentials. Soon we will need a bigger word than *talent* to describe their multifaceted capacities. We all make a special contribution to the whole when we operate from our heart.

I feel that more of humanity is desiring a deeper reassuring connection with their heart's guidance, regardless of what they see in the news and the challenges from unexpected global changes. In my life's review, it was numerous pressing challenges that first scooted me into my *deeper heart connection* for solutions. Like many others, I had the standard tendency to repress my heart's intuitive directions so they wouldn't change my mind-driven ambitions or my off-road choices. After enough emotional pain and setbacks, I finally realized that I could establish a deeper bond with my heart's guidance without pain and regret often being my source of motivation. Pain was not my preferred door to the heart, but I appreciate that it served as a door until I learned that love, respect, and kindness created a much easier entry. With meaningful intention we can all create this life-changing intuitive heart connection. Expanding our care and compassion helps anchor our heart's intuitive connection as a street-wise way of life, not just as a passing trend. We have a limitless supply of love within our heart waiting to hit the street running.

Our inner wisdom is similar to an *app* that's activated as we get still and log into our heart. When our heart energy becomes more present, the clarity of our intuitive messaging increases. Breathing the feeling of love and stillness helps to tune out the *fuzzy* in our intuitive reception and comprehension.

We don't have to be book smart, tech smart, or keep up with all the new spiritual trends to connect with our heart's intuitive guidance and manifest our unrealized gifts and potentials. Many systems now are pointing people to explore their heart's natural guidance for directions. This will continue to move into mainstream acceptance as more people spiritually mature and desire a deeper connection with their true self.

HeartMath and many other systems can inspire, but you don't have to depend on them because you have the guidance within your own heart to lift your spirit and better your life. That's one of the most important themes in my writings; the rest is just filler information that hopefully will inspire people to explore and access the transformational assistance of their own heart's intelligence.

You can use HeartMath and other helpful systems in the same way that many of us used training wheels on our bikes as kids. The training wheels helped us to connect with our sense of balance and self-possibilities but soon *we were riding on our own without the props*. Aim to unfold your own empowerment and the confidence that goes with it; and know that your contribution of love and care to the planet and all life is just as important as any other's. If you feel less than that, know that you can rewrite the beliefs and mindsets that keep you in this lower vibration of self-limitation.

We are not more important than each other. Awareness varies between people because individuals have different timings for personal awareness shifts. This is based on certain life lessons to be experienced so as to free up more of the power of our love and compassion. Comparing our awareness can seduce us into feeling less or more important than others through certain stages of our unfoldment. This is a normal aspect of our ego—the vanity of being special (or not special). Our ego quietly becomes less of an issue as we become more mindful and commit to the ways of love, kindness, and compassion. As we practice putting conscious care into our interactions and keeping our humility refreshed, our forward movement quickens with more flow and less resistance. And especially with less stress.

Purpose

People awakening on the path eventually get curious about their *purpose*, as many now are experiencing. Some people grow up connected with their sense of purpose. Others have searched far and wide for teachers or signs to point them towards their purpose, while many others are not presently concerned with purpose. Early on the path our sense of purpose can bounce around and shape-shift at times. This is because, as our heart's intuition starts to increase, this raises our vibration and awareness, which often changes the course of our desires and directions.

The practice of connecting with our heart's intuitive guidance is a good jump-start for unveiling purpose in perfectly timed stages of our unfoldment. After our mind surrenders the urgency to unveil our purpose, this increases the enjoyable synchronicities that light the way. Our purpose quest becomes more fun and adventuresome when the puzzle pieces show up through unexpected side doors.

If you are someone who follows your passions to discover purpose, it's helpful to understand that passion energy serves the highest bidder—this could be our intuitive heart's desire at times or mostly our ego-driven ambition at other times. Occasionally what we identify as our passion can turn out to be ego-fed energy powered by the mind without the heart's discernment. This is not always the case but check periodically to see if that particular door is ajar. In other cases, our sense of purpose feels aligned with our heart's direction, but the passion seems to be missing—and then the passion unfolds later after we spiritually mature a little more in certain areas of our growth.

After it dawned on me that I had been chasing my heart's purpose mostly with my mind, I finally released the glamor of being too caught up in purpose-browsing and learned to trust in my heart's guidance to help connect the dots. My heart revealed this to me: Learning to listen to my heart's guidance was *the most important step* in manifesting my purpose, regardless of how my vocational choices and life played out.

Establishing more trust in my heart's wisdom created a baseline which made it easier for my internal and external purpose to naturally align with each other through time. My passion and sense of mission increased as I matured in the way I responded to life's lessons. I was shown that another key aspect of my purpose was learning to use my heart's intelligence to help navigate the transition between self-centeredness and an expanded love for the whole. I began the process of sorting out who I am from who I thought I was. I saw that to become my true self would involve learning to free the dynamic love that I felt inside but couldn't fully express, because of my resistance to loving myself.

Years ago, the term self-love put me off, as it sounded too self-centered. My perception changed as I realized that loving myself was simply practicing natural heart qualities such as: gratitude, patience, being kinder and more compassionate with myself, including my heart in decisions and choices, being mindful and non-judgmental of my inner and external environments, releasing the vanity around failing to get everything perfect, etc. These practices bring forth the essence of our true self.

Our true self *is already perfect*; it doesn't require fixing—it's like a perfect orange that's full of sunshine but we have to take the peeling off to free up the juice. We advance as we peel off the old perceptions and behaviors that no longer benefit us and that keep people from getting along with each other. Doing this reveals the light and gifts from our true being.

For many years now, the external manifestation of my purpose has been to make available anything I've learned that might facilitate others who choose to connect with their heart's intelligent guidance. Living from our heart connects the puzzle pieces of our purpose and aligns us with our personal empowerment and fulfillment.

Conscience

Most of us have heard this statement repeated throughout life: "Let your conscience be your guide." Our conscience signals us at times, like a text message, offering an opportunity to course-correct our attitudes or actions. Usually when someone says, "My conscience is bothering me," it's when their thoughts, feelings, or actions are out of sync with the integrity of their true nature—their heart of hearts. Though our conscience doesn't force us to comply with its suggestions, it affords us a chance to think twice, and then twice again, before continuing with certain ego-driven notions that don't include our heart's assessment of the circumstances. Conscience is an intuitive vibration that serves as a reminder of our integrity, dignity, and care; it's a reference of intuitive assessment, prompting us to be more conscious in discerning our choices and actions. Our conscience is a friendly, yet occasionally firm reminder of who we really are when we are dipping too low into "who we are not."

I wish the Designer would have given people's conscience a louder voice because some of the choices I made in my twenties were proof that I could hardly hear it at all. Many people are commenting to us that their conscience is getting louder and clearer. This will increase and become more obvious as these changing times continue, and as we connect more with our heart and the care that we are about.

Balancing Masculine and Feminine Energy Within

It's often a mystery why many of our practices and intentions for self-transformation tend to fizzle. Part of the reason is because of the lack of balance and partnership between the masculine and feminine energy within each of us. Each person is a combination of masculine and feminine frequencies, regardless of their gender. For example, our *feminine* side is more sensitive to our intuitive guidance and our *masculine* energy is important for helping to step down and anchor this guidance into day-to-day behavior. This is only one example of balanced partnering between our masculine and feminine qualities.

Transformational benefits of balancing our masculine and feminine energy include a clearer connection with our heart's intelligent communication, an increased capacity to heal and maintain our system, and more. Our masculine and feminine energies (frequencies) shape our lives. Our heart's intelligence can help to unfold the balance and cooperation between these two energies that constantly fashion our outcomes and decide our peace.

The imbalance of our masculine and feminine energy results in many of the mental and emotional limitations that hinder our potential for being the best that we can be. Usually we are top-heavy on one side or the other. This imbalance weakens our self-assessment capacity, causing us to overplay our strengths so as to hide our weaknesses from others and ourselves. This is only one of many different play-outs that spin from masculine and feminine energetic imbalance. More people are feeling a nudge to find balance within, even if they aren't sure what they are trying to balance. Inner balance is a foundation for the next level of consciousness that humanity is progressively shifting towards. Here is an oversimplified view of a potential play-out:

As we progressively balance our masculine and feminine energy, then our spirit kicks it up a notch and starts releasing the gifts of our higher potentials into our day-to-day interactions. Our heart's intuitive guidance helps us use these gifts to unfold the most fulfilling version of our life. Along with this comes the compassion and desire to facilitate others to do the same.

Through countless generations, masculine energies have dominated the planet and repressed our much needed feminine qualities and sensitivities within both the male and female genders. However, that page is turning and a new one is being written. It starts the real-life chapter on the transformational benefits of balance and cooperation. Feminine energies (within men and women) are coming into their rightful, long-awaited moment. More men than ever are becoming heart-vulnerable and awakening to the benefits of balancing their masculine and feminine frequencies. They are recognizing this is a missing piece in their personal empowerment process. Women are moving at god-speed in balancing these energies so that their feminine strengths and qualities can be heard, respected, and equally considered. This process includes the challenge of not getting too dominant in male frequencies from overcompensation as this can create a hindrance in the personal transformation process. Staying close to the heart can help to guide and anchor this delicate balance.

Accessing our heart's intelligence can make these balancing adjustments much friendlier and more effective. As our mind and emotions advance into cooperative alignment with our heart, this naturally brings balance and adjustment in our masculine and feminine energies with much more ease and grace. Some people are born with more aspects of masculine/feminine balance. That wasn't me. I was a little male-heavy. In the neighborhood I was raised in as a boy, it would have been fighting words if someone had told me that I needed to wake up "the girl in me" to become a balanced person. However, my ego vanity softened through the years.

Global Rangers Skit:

"Alright men, let's saddle up and ride through the planet to straighten out this global stress mess."

"Should we take the ladies?" someone shouted.

"Oh, they already left in a gallop—they were first to sense humanity's needs and are well on their way to assist!"

"Well gentlemen, we better get moving to see if there's anything left that we can still feel like we are in charge of!"

Ego

Our ego is not the boogie man, and with patience and inner guidance it can be transformed into its higher-vibrational purpose. Qualifying life through the heart transforms the frequency of our ego nature and brings it into resonance with the vibration of our true self. For most of us, our ego in its lower vibration has created problems along the way that we've blamed on others and life. Ego often pouts when it wants something different than what it's getting. Our heart's guidance can help to bring about a natural maturing process of our ego nature at each stage of our increased awareness. This is much more effective for taming the ego than shaming it or blaming it.

When I first got on the path, I would become spiritually congested from criticizing and hammering on my ego like a woodpecker, thinking I was on a fast track to self-mastery (while hoping God was watching my moves). I eventually learned that putting too much pressure on ego supervision comes from the ego itself. Our intentions to tame our ego can seem noble. Yet, if they are mind-driven intentions without the heart's deeper discernment, they create stress from constant setbacks—especially from trying to spiritually advance too quickly like the rabbit, without the wisdom and patience of the turtle.

As we commit to making peace with our ego without condemning it, then our heart's coaching will eventually transform it into the ways it serves our highest best, and in perfect timing. Don't throw your ego out with the bath water. The ego becomes transformed as it advances through the stages of reducing self-centeredness. Once it senses our commitment is heart-solid, our ego will surrender to the strength of our inner dignity. All aspects of our nature, including our ego, are part of our divinity and play important roles in the process of becoming our empowered best. Love and appreciate them all.

Happiness

There is a lot of recent research and books written on happiness and even a country (Bhutan) that measures "Gross National Happiness." I realize it's hard not to feel that happiness is sourced from the outside—people, places, and things. I embarked on an endless search to find peace and state-of-the-art happiness until I realized that my mind was searching for something that my heart was more qualified at providing. The mind is wonderful, but when it comes to a deep-dive assessment regarding what will really make us happy, we are smart to engage our heart's wisdom and intelligence. The mind and emotions may *pout* a little when we ask our heart's discernment to help run the show, but eventually our mind will savor the idea of having such a grounded mentor as the intelligent heart.

At times people can experience long, empty spaces between really being happy and just getting by. Opening our heart more in our interactions with others helps fill these empty spaces with care and deeper connections. This is a higher-vibrational practice, and a fundamental step towards personal happiness and fulfillment. As we practice raising the vibration of our love rather than chasing happiness through people, stimulation, and stuff (even if it's good stuff), we will discover that increased happiness is a natural occurrence *that just shows up when we are qualifying life through our heart*.

Happiness is a higher vibration that we often pursue from a lower-vibrational attitude and we can't quite catch it by the tail. Happy periods can be extended or fragmented, based on how much lower frequency energy we process or store (such as fear, insecurity, image challenges, hurts, resentments, etc.). These lower frequency energies create predictable glitches in our natural flow of happiness. Then we try to fill the void with behaviors that spark moments of feeling good but have a short and costly shelf life.

When we achieve a vibration of happiness that doesn't have to be baited or conditional, then everything else is an add-on, not a depend-on (which is the mother of disappointments). For example, true grounded happiness is not dependent on how well an event goes. True happiness remains if the event gets canceled or the event is uneventful. (Even if we have to breathe-out a few times to reset.)

It's counter-productive to apply for continuous happiness without clearing out lower-vibrational attitudes that can't share the same space. Happiness is an inside job—which is a game changer when we discover this. View happiness as a high-end spiritual perk that we learn to unleash from within, and not make life an endless pilgrimage trying to find it.

Let's hold compassion in our hearts for the millions of people who don't have the luxury to be concerned about happiness, as they are deeply pressed in the survival mode from wars, viruses, natural disasters, starvation, abuse, etc. We can't change this picture overnight, but our love and compassion can help in ways that we can't see. No genuine love is ever wasted even if we can't always monitor and track its fine workings. Better times for the whole are unfolding—and we are the transformational engineers.

CHAPTER 8

THE DIFFERENCE BETWEEN CARE AND OVERCARE

By Doc Childre

As we spiritually mature into our higher potentials, increased care comes with it. Caring more is a most valid way for love to be stepped down into practical applications. This would solve and prevent many problems that we unconsciously create and repeat.

For the next few paragraphs I'll comment on the difference between care and overcare. Overcare is when our initial feelings of care about something or someone turn into obsessive worry, anxiety, or projecting the worst—this usually escalates into emotional depletion and the obvious stress load that follows. Our care is one of our highest assets, but when our care turns into overcare, it drains our energy and our health bears the consequences. Managing our care nurtures us and others, while overcare hinders our effectiveness with energy-draining mind loops even when our intentions are well-meaning.

We know that numerous caregivers experience a high rate of energetic burnout from not being able to manage the energies of their care. That's understandable because managing our care has a predictable learning curve and it's not an easy task for people who care deeply. It's part of an emotional maturing process in learning the economy of balanced care.

Below are some typical areas where overcare can overwhelm us at times, lowering our vibration while draining our energy:

- Work
- Relationships
- Money
- Diet
- Children
- Parents
- Health
- Past regrets
- How we look
- How we feel
- Future security
- How we will come out
- Feeling lack
- Comparisons
- What people think of us (and what we privately think of them)
- Learning new technology

Many issues on the list are often draining our energy at the same time, reducing our resilience and our capacity to feel good, while compromising our health and vitality. Then we wonder why we don't feel like our full-blown self.

A stealthy ingredient in overcare is its seductive power to *justify itself*, while leaving us blindsided to its energy-sapping consequences. With practice, we can cue up our intuition to alert us when overcare begins to invade our feelings and perceptions. The practice of identifying and deleting overcare can save a pivotal amount of energy and health risk along the way.

Eliminating overcare does not reduce our care; it strengthens the effectiveness of our care by bringing it into balance and coherent alignment with our heart. Any time our outgoing energy is balanced, we are smarter on our feet. View overcare (unmanaged care) as a thriving emotional virus, hidden by society's unconscious agreement that overcare is *not accountable*. With our heart's intuitive guidance and commitment, we can free ourselves from the seductive stress that overcare and constant worry bring us.

An excessive (obsessive) amount of overcare and emotional turbulence can unconsciously stream from trying to navigate the learning curve of new software, computers, smartphones, or other "must-have" devices. *Yes, they are helpful*, but that doesn't expunge the cumulative stress deficits accrued from the anxiety of having to keep up with it all, especially if you don't have a knack for it. A balancing gesture would be to occasionally do a reality check and ask: *Are we consumers of our technology or are we consumed by our technology? Are we the programmers of our gadgets or are we pawns of our gadgets?* When addiction creeps in, we become the pawns and the gadgets become our master. Finding balance in all things is a heart-intelligent practice in these accelerated times, especially when technology is fixing to explode into science fiction-type potentials. Have fun but stay in charge, or you become the pawn. There's no gray, you know.

Distinguishing Care vs. Overcare

At first, trying to distinguish the difference between balanced care and overcare can seem complicated. This is because when we are in overcare, we can tend to feel *that's when we are caring the most*. Many issues we start to care about morph into worry. Excessive worry is a classic example of when overcare is fooling us into thinking that it's *effective care*. In our heart, most of us know that free-to-roam worry eventuates into personal energy deficits and compromises our well-being. *(If we truly believed that excessive worry really helped us, we would encourage our friends and children to go find a corner and worry each time life's challenges come up.)*

You may ask how can people not go into worry and anxiety over some things or situations that put others or themselves in harms way? There are serious things that happen in life that amp up our concern—but most overcare energy drain is about things and issues that often don't even matter that much. Yet we're addicted to the habit or drama of overcare. These are especially the situations where managing our care would be effective. Overcare is a deeply imprinted human tendency that's handed down through each generation. It's like a virus that can only be cured through *self*-adjustment. Others can't do it for us. There's no vaccine; however we don't need one, because overcare is nothing that we can't handle with a little conscious focus along with our heart's commitment to practice. Observe yourself for a few days and see how often you can catch *overcare* occupying your mind and feelings regarding yourself, others, or issues. When you find yourself in worry, anxiety, or distress from overcare try the following exercise.

Overcare Exercise

1. While breathing in a relaxed pace, pretend you are breathing through your heart or chest area and imagine calming your mind and emotions with your breath. (Calm emotions help to create a space that enables intuitive access for clearer discernment and choices when evaluating situations.)

2. Once you've calmed your mental and emotional vibrations, then commit to repeating this breathing exercise whenever you find yourself fading back into overcare. Sometimes after a few rounds of doing this, you'll find your energies more balanced and easier to manage.

3. As you practice, don't be concerned if it doesn't work every time. It won't. (You'll get plenty more chances.) Being genuine strengthens the power of your heart's intention.

Approach this exercise with *ease*, not force. With practice, you will become more conscious of when you are overcaring, and often you can *just stop it on the spot* and bring your energy back to balance. Practice increases the strength for actualizing intentions that otherwise fizzle before they land. Heart energy added to any practice brings fortitude and resilience into our intentions, especially when our commitments start to shrink.

This simple exercise is not just for overcare and worry; it's helpful for any stressful challenge or situation that calls for clearer discernment without the emotional override. Remember that worry is one of the highest contributors to overcare because it seems so "legal" and normal. I've found that understanding and managing *overcare* is one of the most forward-moving steps we can take in our personal transformation process.

Often, we get an intuitive inspiration to change and replace overcare or other nonsupportive emotional patterns. However, *inspiration* quickly wilts like a leftover party balloon if we don't "act on it" much sooner than later. Inspiration self-sustains as we use it. As we become more skilled at this, we learn to move forward with our intuitive nudges while the heat from inspiration is still warm. This multiplies our potential for achieving our aim as it raises us above the vibration of overcare and our predictable resistances. Inspiration is a spirit-filled moment. It's *a packet of free energetic initiative—with a timer on it*. As we move forward with the first nudge of Inspiration, we can beat the human tendency to waste that intuitive gift from our heart. I've found that sometimes it's many moons before certain needed inspirations return, if we miss acting on them on the first pass. It's about learning the economy of spirit.

We *can* reduce and change stress producing patterns as we put our heart into it—like we tell kids to do when committing to something important. I'll comment on fear in the next few pages because worry unattended often grows into fear, which is the biggest collective challenge across the planet.

Addressing Fear

It's often hard to remember that we have the choice to apply emotional regulation when triggered by fear from personal matters or global concerns, such as terrorism, civil unrest, viruses, climate change, etc. Many of us have learned that our health and well-being are jeopardized if we don't practice some form of inner balance when constantly challenged by fear—whether our fear is real or not. Panic and fear put a haze around our sensible assessments and choices by numbing our higher reasoning capacity. More people are becoming tired of fear having the power to disassemble their emotional constitution and self-security.

Most of us have wished to manage fear for a long time, yet often nothing changes until we step forward and put our *heart's* commitment behind our mind's intentions. We frequently engage just our mind to resolve challenges that instead require the sensitive guidance of our heart's intelligence. The mind often trips over itself while impatiently rushing towards quick fixes, leaving a trail of setbacks and restarts. Our mind working in alignment with our heart's suggestions creates an intuitive draw for information or effective steps for managing fear or other unwanted behavioral patterns.

Heart-Based Practices for Reducing Fear

From experience, I have learned the importance of approaching fear with *ease* and *self-compassion* rather than with mind struggle. Impatience sent many of my fear-reducing intentions straight to the trash basket until I learned that *patience* is also a *must* for transforming fear, not an option. When our intuitive reasoning capacity becomes restricted from fear, this causes our self-security alarm to go off and create a powerful inner distortion which we call panic, overwhelm, etc. You can reduce this by placing importance on *slowing down the vibrations of your mind and emotions*; this helps to reduce the charge or intensity of fear or anxiety. It can be done by slow breathing while imagining your breath entering through your heart area. An effective way to learn to manage emotional intensity is to first practice on smaller emotions such as frustration, irritation, impatience, and such. Reducing mental and emotional intensity is a gateway to intuitive sensitivity for wiser choices and solutions.

Below are a few practices you may already be using for managing fear and anxiety:

Don't try to *stop* fear; simply commit to increasingly reduce fear *a little at a time* (with ease, not push). Don't put a timer on the process. Release self-judgment or negative feelings towards your fear as this creates more resistance. Know that fear becomes more negotiable as we reduce the extra drama created in self-talk and imaginary projections with dim outcomes. I did this habitually until I realized that my mind was addicted to over-thinking the aspects of fear—trying to be too complex in assessing my feelings (like boy Freud). The more we amplify fear with drama, the more we empower the fears we wish to eliminate. Most of us already know this—until the fear pops up again.

If watching the news is a trigger for you, simply practice breathing in the feeling of calm and emotional balance while watching the news. *As you breathe, see yourself maintaining care and compassion for humanity's challenges without taking on their pain and fear.* This doesn't mean that you care less.

If the news seems too hard to deal with at times, then know that it's okay not to watch it at all. We have to be honest with ourselves in deciding if following the news supports or compromises our well-being based on our individual nature and constitution. Without truly learning dispassion, many people would probably fare better by not constantly watching the news. I often choose to watch global news because it stokes the fire of my commitment to have compassion for the fear and suffering experienced throughout the planet. With practice, the mind and heart can learn to process dispassion and compassion at the same time. Nowadays, a lot of the population has to watch the news for updates on continuously changing guidelines related to a virus, extreme weather, health concerns, civil unrest, etc. Like many issues, the news has its assets and its deficits. Use your own heart to decide what's best for you.

The practice that helped me the most to reduce fear is this:

In prayer or meditation, I would visualize love from my heart streaming into my mind and into all my cells to change my old fear imprints. While breathing, I would hold a conscious intention in my heart to change my old programs of fear and anxiety into feelings of *intelligent concern* (managed concern)—which is a much more objective and less stressful attitude than the feeling of fear.

Fear disempowers us—whereas the attitude of *intelligent concern* can handle stepped-up mental intensity with clearer discernment and choices, leaving us in charge and more attuned to intuitive direction. Intelligent concern is a health-conscious replacement attitude for fear. Make a heart commitment to practice befriending fear and reducing the feeling to *intelligent concern* (managed concern) to whatever threatens your inner or outer security.

Practicing first on less intense fears quickly strengthened my capacity to objectively shift and dissipate some of my deeper fears and anxieties. As you practice reducing and transforming fear, realize that small steps are wise steps because they create a balanced pace which draws less discouragement. Also remember to practice with patience and self-compassion and allow for slipups without self-judgment and resignation. Approach it with ease, without urgency or self-doubt.

These few paragraphs don't come close to addressing the endless situations and circumstances that can trigger our fears. People have searched for ages trying to find that "fix all, fear-eraser." Many other helpful instructions are available if you research books and information on the subject. If you desire it from your heart, you will draw to you additional information that can help you replace your fears with increased self-security.

Helping Children Maintain Their Heart Connection

One of the best things parents can do for children especially during challenging times is to practice maintaining their own heart connection. The pandemic impacted children and teens with social isolation, homeschooling, mask-wearing, and uncertainty about their future. At the time of this writing, according to a study out of Calgary University, one in five youth are experiencing clinically elevated anxiety symptoms and one in four adolescents globally are experiencing clinically elevated depression symptoms.[1]

Often when small kids are distressed, unhappy, or experiencing a tantrum, we instinctively redirect their energy by giving them a toy or loving attention, and almost instantly they can totally change their frequency pitch (vibration) to calmness, joy, elation, or contentment (higher pitch emotions). A primary reason that young children often transform compressive emotions quickly is because in their early years of development they are still connected to the higher frequencies of their natural heart attributes, such as uncomplicated love, transparency, lack of prejudice, and their *superpower to release and move on*. Their minds are not yet entrained to the countless lower vibration societal mindsets and habits that often overshadow their heart's higher feelings and choices.

The collective consciousness is slowly awakening to the need to educate children in the difference between their mind and heart and how to maintain their heart connection in their interactions. This usually starts by teaching younger children appreciation, kindness, sharing, compassionate care for others who are sad or feeling low, etc. It's especially important for young children to learn how to go to their heart space for comfort and guidance when they're stressed and emotionally overloaded. Older children can learn to connect with their heart's intuitive guidance amidst societal stress and society's hard and fast entrainment to overstimulation, overcare, ambition, competition, and techno-mania.

One of the biggest obstructions in a child's development (but not intentional) is when parents assume that they always know best regarding what their kids should be and do as they become adults. Millions of children end up playing out the dreams of their parent's ideal personifications. To most parents in these situations, it seems normal and motivated by care. It is care—but often care that doesn't include the sensitivity to the way the child is natured. This unintentionally tries to force-fit a child into molds that don't fit. Guidance is important, yet guidance occasionally needs an awareness-upgrade that's more inclusive of the consequences it generates. Most everyone realizes that, for a long time now, children around the world are born with more awareness than previous generations. This increased awareness can cause resistance and separation in teens when they are pressured in directions that their deeper heart feels are not right for them—especially regarding vocation and relationship choices. Updated guidance models are available that can prevent much stress and emotional resistance in children from spirit repression. Guidance needs to include an awareness of their individual nature and their deeper heart's inclinations and desires. New consciousness regarding this is on the rise, yet there's much left to be done to change old-school guidance patterns.

With compassion, I encourage parents to be proactive in becoming more informed about effective new models and information regarding child-rearing. Most parents are doing the best they can with the time constraints they have. But it's time for us all to upgrade our awareness because in our heart of hearts, we want our children and young adults to become *who they truly are*. Parents also need to have compassion for themselves, as keeping up with children's accelerated awareness is one of the harder challenges, especially in these times. I compassionately understand the extra commitment this takes. I realize it's even harder now for adults to stay balanced and sort out their next steps.

Our younger generation's increasing awareness will eventually help to change society's conflicting lower-vibrational mindsets that have cost so many lives and generated ongoing hatred, trauma, and retribution. New generations won't tend to support the intolerance and separation that block harmonious connections and caring interactions among all people. Our younger generation is already finding its way towards becoming more effective in inspiring the need for a global change of heart.

NOTES

1. Racine, N. et al. *Global prevalence of depressive and anxiety symptoms in children and adolescents during COVID-19: A meta-analysis. JAMA pediatrics* (2021).

CHAPTER 9

COMPASSION: THE NEED OF THE TIMES

By Doc Childre

Compassion increases in effectiveness as we mature in practicing the core qualities of the heart, such as unconditional love, allowance, acceptance, and an unattached desire for the highest outcome for all concerned. Cultivating these heart qualities strengthens our compassion and frees it to serve the highest best. True compassion benefits the sender and receiver, though we can't always see the ways it nurtures and heals or makes it easier to adjust to tougher situations we experience.

Many of us have felt drained and stressed on occasion from what we thought was *giving compassion*. This energy drain and depletion can be triggered especially from unbalanced empathetic care. Empathy can produce strong feelings of care but often comes with tentacles that create over-attachment to what we care about.

Compassion is one of the highest supportive energies of love. I used to think it was for fixing others. We can support each other with our love and compassion, but people have to do their own fixing from within. I was a dedicated "Mr. Fix-all" until I learned that people have to make their own adjustments or else challenges keep repeating—sometimes in different arrangements, and sometimes in much harder circumstances. Often the problems we rush to fix for others are their growth opportunities for learning to connect more deeply within their own heart and soul for direction and solutions.

Learning to *balance* our empathetic interactions is a big step towards understanding the tone of true compassion. Compassion is an unconditional love that supports the highest outcome for others without depleting our personal reservoir of energy. Whereas unmanaged empathy, sympathetic attachment, and "tired-care" are the rocks to look behind when we feel drained from extending what we felt was our heart's compassion. One reason that compassion is misunderstood is that for ages, people have used the term "compassion" as a convenient *cover-all* word for what is often sympathy, empathy, pity, or excessive worry. More people are being prompted from within to gain a deeper understanding of compassion, since compassion tops the list of what would benefit humanity most in these transitional times.

Compassion is a powerful core frequency within our heart, but in most cases it takes practice to feel love and care for people in extreme stress without becoming overly-identified with their challenges (a learning curve for all of us). One expression of true compassion is when we can hold love and light for others in dark moments, without draining our own battery and joining them in the dark.

More about Empathy

Since compassion is so often confused with empathy, I feel it could be helpful to restate a few points that set these two expressions of care apart. As mentioned earlier, sensitivity to other's pain points often triggers feelings of compassion and empathetic care; however, the effectiveness of our care diminishes rapidly when we over-attach mentally and emotionally to their issues. Empathy can sense the suffering of others yet can be managed to maintain balance and energetic composure within its care.

News stories, children's challenges, other people's health issues, etc. can elicit our empathetic responses which, without management, can trigger a continuous drain throughout our whole system even if we feel like we are "kind of in charge." Empathy starts out as an asset, yet it can become a source of misery if we don't find our balance with it. A reality moment is when we realize (not just intellectually, but *really* get it) that unmanaged empathy can produce continuous energy deficits that far outweigh the "good" we think we are providing to others. Unnecessary aging comes with this quandary.

The following is a standard outcome that most of us have read about or experienced from unmanaged empathy:

*On the edge of burnout, we end up livid with ourselves for sinking too deep into others' challenges, or the world's problems, and then we get angry because there's nobody to blame but ourselves (though we give it a good try). It gets worse as we remember that we learned our lesson the last time this happened—and here we are again. This is often followed by self-judgment and self-reduction until we get too worn down to even do that. Then we stressfully re-gather ourselves over a period of time and start all over with new self-care commitments, feeling like we've **really** learned our lesson this time....*

We can change the ending to these stories of self-generated ambushes by paying more attention to intuitive feelings that signal us when our empathetic care becomes unbalanced from *over-attachment and self-depletion*. Our heart's intuitive feelings often provide warnings before self-depletion sets in, but we can often fall short on taking action because we think over-emotional identity to what we care about is justified. At times our mind is good at diverting us from our heart's wiser suggestions.

Like many others, my heart intuition was blocked by my mind's misinterpretation of empathy. I thought living on the edge of burnout from serving others was virtuous and noble. I felt it was proof of my self-sacrifice "to share the light and spread the good" like a little knight. (Picture a knight in shining ignorance on a mission to *fix everyone*, whatever the personal cost—that was me at age twenty-five.) Much of that experience was from young-buck ego vanity, mixed with sincere, yet *unbalanced* empathetic care. I've moved on since then after learning the same lesson, repeatedly. But I still closely monitor the difference between empathy and balanced care. It stays high on my personal list of self-care maintenance practices.

Remember, empathy itself is not the source of energy drains; it's the unintentional mishandling of empathy that drains and taxes our well-being. Our hearts have the capacity to maintain energetic detachment and emotional equability, but this requires a little genuine practice to instate. It's one of the most valuable gifts we can give ourselves. Balanced empathy can nurture and serve others without serving us up with it. Learning the difference between lower empathetic attachment and balanced care can help dissolve most of the problems around empathy—and help us mature in the understanding of true compassion and its effectiveness. This practice may be helpful in balancing empathy:

Practice watching some recorded movie scenes where the characters are experiencing a medium amount of physical or emotional pain that creates a challenging sympathetic or empathetic feeling in you. As you watch, breathe in a relaxed way and practice detaching yourself from the emotional over-identification.

If you do this enough times you will eventually find a place within yourself where you can regulate your feelings. You will start to realize that you can actually genuinely care about what is going on without it pulling you into it.

The advantage of watching the scenes several times in a row is that it gives you more chances to experiment with finding that *inner switch* which regulates your emotional output. Practicing with movie scenes gives you a jump start on learning dispassion and intentional composure, which help with learning true compassion. These types of practices are often used by first responders to learn to maintain emotional composure as they respond to car wrecks, catastrophes, and such. This skill can be developed. Know in your heart that maintaining your emotional composure, without suffering with people in distress, doesn't mean that you care less for them. Your care and compassion are actually more effective.

Compassionate Latitude

Compassionate latitude is a heart quality that realizes most people are doing the best they can based on their stress overload, anxiety, and the strained thinking so many are experiencing these days. Latitude is the consideration and understanding that we all fall short at times in our choices, words, or actions, especially when enduring stress from challenges that others aren't aware of. Compassionate latitude increases patience and encourages a deeper understanding of another's situation.

Practicing compassionate latitude with each other quickly begins to reduce and prevent stress build-up from stored anger, judgments, and resentments. This is so important for maintaining balance and resilience during pressing times of change and unpredictability. It's time to skip the drama, reduce judgments and resentments, and move on. Here's an exercise that can help.

Compassionate Latitude Exercise

1. Start with quiet breathing while radiating feelings of care for someone or something you appreciate. This helps to shift your energy from the mind to your heart.

2. Next, ponder situations where you could give others more compassionate latitude (e.g. at home, at work, and especially while sorting out miscommunications, etc.)

3. As you breathe, imagine yourself reducing judgments, infuriated responses, and lack of tolerance with compassionate latitude (e.g. attitudes of deeper care, kindness, patience, understanding, and tolerance). Practicing several days in a row helps to anchor this valuable habit.

Another helpful exercise is each day find situations where you can replace judgments and reactions with compassionate latitude.

More on Self-Compassion

Self-compassion is an advanced step in anyone's personal empowerment and self-care practices. At first people tend to respond awkwardly when it's suggested they feel compassion for themselves—it can seem a little self-serving, out of place, undeserved, unspiritual, etc. These attitudes come from handed-down entrainment from old belief systems that don't serve us anymore. Self-compassion has been on the back burner too long, and now it's time to seize the moment and take advantage of its transformational benefits. To have compassion for yourself is not an act of selfishness; it's an act of intelligence, heart intelligence.

Don't confuse self-compassion with pity-party-type emotions; it's a transformative vibration from our heart that nurtures us with nonjudgmental acceptance and a deeper understanding of our self. Practicing this form of self-care is especially helpful when transitioning through situations that require time for healing and emotional adjustment. If we have physical or emotional challenges, self-compassion intuitively guides and supports us through the best ways to handle our issues or situations. However, self-compassion is not just for challenging times as it could seem. It's a regenerative energy that serves as a tonic for our cells and our operating system.

Self-compassion is a higher-vibrational frequency sourced from the love and power of our heart and spirit. We obviously think compassion is beneficial or else we wouldn't automatically gush it out to others, pets, or suffering around the world, etc. Why wouldn't we do this for ourselves? See self-compassion as *a powerful self-maintenance type of care*. This process gets easier once you understand it is just another self-care practice, like putting salve on a sore arm. Here's an exercise you can try:

Self-Compassion Exercise

1. To practice self-compassion, simply get quiet somewhere and imagine creating an inner spa.

2. Imagine breathing self-compassion and positive energy into your mental/emotional nature and into

your physical cells. Most importantly, do this from the heart as it connects directly with the healing and renewing qualities from your spirit.

Self-compassion takes a little practice, but today's transitional times call for these types of practices because of compassion's restorative benefits to our mental, emotional, and physical nature.

....

Compassion is a most powerful and intelligent frequency within the love spectrum. As we unconditionally express compassion, it intuitively chooses its own way to administer its care based on a sensitive attunement to the higher need of the whole. Pure compassion is not tethered to our agendas; it's free to weave its magic, sometimes visibly yet often unseen, but never wasted as it nurtures all within its radiance. True compassion supports the highest-best outcome, which is not always what our personality would choose or understand. Unconditional love sets the tone for true compassion. As our human intelligence spirals to the next station of enlightenment, then collective compassion will become the foundational vibration for amplifying the connection with our soul and source as they stream love and healing through our human experience. Compassion is transformational love and care manifesting in the most ripened state of effectiveness for the whole.

– Doc

CHAPTER 10

HEART COHERENCE: ACCESS TO HEART INTELLIGENCE

By Rollin McCraty

Many people know what it feels like to be in a state of inner harmony, where heart and mind are working in sync. We flow through challenges with ease and have genuine connections with others. It's easy to love this experience of inner harmony, but often times it happens by chance, rather than by design or intention. Wouldn't it be nice to be able to create and experience this alignment more often, in our day-to-day communications, projects, and challenges?

So what empowers our ability to create more balance and harmony in ourselves, our relationships, our work, and in how we handle our challenges? Through over twenty years of applied research at the HeartMath Institute, we identified a physiological state we researchers call *heart coherence* that supports a balanced partnership in the interactions between our heart, mind, emotions. Practicing techniques that increase our heart coherence has been shown in numerous studies to enhance health, well-being, relationships, and performance, in a broad range of contexts and cultures.

To help demystify the term *coherence*, let's use a simple analogy. Imagine being in meditation or prayer and being constantly interrupted by intruding thoughts, feelings, worries, mind loops, or even good ideas, all of which can disrupt and scatter the focus and effectiveness of our intentions. This creates a type of incoherence or internal noise. On the other hand, increasing our heart coherence before or during prayer or meditation helps us sustain and maintain a more genuine, heartfelt focus which translates into increased intuitive guidance and personal effectiveness. Getting into this state of coherence helps to align and coordinate our thoughts and emotions with our heart's intelligence, so that mixed agendas or mixed signals don't scramble our minds. Incoherence is like static on a radio station we are listening to, whereas internal coherence better "tunes us in" to the station and we get a much clearer signal.

A common dictionary definition of coherence is "the quality of being logically integrated, consistent and intelligible," as in a coherent statement or in the efficiency and effectiveness of words and actions. Another definition is "the orderly and harmonious relationships among the various parts of something, whether a living system such as a human being or the cosmos." The term coherence always implies connectedness among parts of a system, along with stability and efficient energy utilization within the system. It also implies that the system as a whole is greater than the sum of its individual parts.

In our bodies, a type of coherence occurs when our rhythmic systems, such as our breathing, blood pressure, and heart rhythms, are in sync with each other. If the term coherence still seems difficult to understand, you might think of it like an orchestra where there are many different instruments being played, yet all have to be resonant and in sync or in alignment.

Our bodies have many glands and organ systems that have to work together in a harmonious, coordinated, and synchronized dance for us to be able to sustain health[1,2]. In fact, this type of coherence has been proposed as the quality that makes life possible.[1] Not only is the term coherence used to describe harmony in our physical processes, but also in our mental and emotional composure and ability to adapt to life's daily challenges.

Coherence can also be applied to social settings. *Social coherence* is reflected as a stable, harmonious alignment of the relationships in a group (family, sports, leadership team, organization, etc.). Social coherence enables an efficient flow and utilization of energy and communication, all of which are necessary for optimal group cohesion and cooperative action. When the relationships in a group are discordant and the group members are not getting along with each other, this typically results in dysfunction, instability, more mistakes, and poor performance.

At HeartMath, we have studied personal and social coherence in great detail, as well as how personal heart coherence facilitates social and global coherence. Here's a simple scientific overview of personal heart coherence. The next two chapters explain social and global coherence.

Heart Coherence

Heart coherence refers to an optimal state in which the mind and emotions are in sync and in alignment with the energetic heart's intuitive guidance. Physiologically, it is a specific state that can be seen and measured in the heart's rhythmic activity. There is a lot taking place inside our bodies when we're in a physiological state of heart coherence (much more than I can detail here). For example, there is increased harmony and synchronization among the neurons in the higher-level centers in the brain; increased synchronization in the neural activity (communication) between the heart and brain; increased harmony in the activity of the autonomic nervous system (ANS); and increased activity in the parasympathetic nervous system (PNS), (also known as vagal nerve activity).

Importantly, the heart-coherent state is associated with greater emotional balance and stability, increased access to intuition, and improved mental functions (ability to focus, memory, reaction times, coordination, etc.).

As mentioned in Chapter 3, research has also revealed that the physical heart has its own nervous system. Neuro-cardiologists call it the intrinsic cardiac nervous system and nicknamed it the heart-brain.[3] University research on the structure and functions of this heart-brain has significantly enhanced HeartMath research as it provides more clearly the anatomical details of how the heart and brain are in constant communication. It helps expand understanding of how the activity of the heart influences brain centers involved in perception, cognitive performance, and emotional experience.[4-7]

An important measure that provides researchers a unique window into the communication occurring between heart and brain and into the activity occurring in the ANS is called heart rhythm analysis or heart rate variability analysis, or simply HRV.

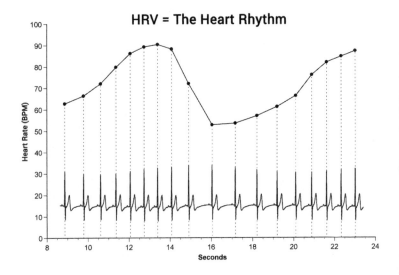

Figure 1 - This graph shows an example of the beat-to-beat changes occurring over a 24-second period. The trace on the bottom is the ECG and the dots on the top line are the instantaneous heart rate. The line that connects the dots forms the heart rhythm pattern. The upslope in the line represents an increase in heart rate, meaning there is a series of heartbeats that are speeding up (less time between heartbeats) while the downslope represents a decrease in heart rate, meaning there is a series of heartbeats slowing down (more time between heartbeats).

Heart Rate Variability

We all know that heart rate refers to how many times the heart beats in a minute (BPM). Heart Rate Variability (HRV) refers to the naturally occurring changes in the timing between each and every heartbeat *(see Figure 1)*. It is this beat-to-beat variation that creates the heart's rhythm. When we look closely, we typically can see a pattern where the heart rate increases over a series of heartbeats then slows over the next series of heartbeats, as in Figure 1. Much of this naturally occurring variability is due to our heart and brain communicating with each other through the autonomic nervous system. This variability occurs all the time, even when we are sleeping or resting.

A good amount of amplitude in our variability (the distance between the peak and trough in our HRV waveform) is a marker of good health. The amplitude of HRV is also considered a measure of our resilience and well-being. In fact, many studies find that having an optimal level of variability for our age is related to our ability to be flexible and adaptable to changing social situations and to life's challenges, both big and small.[7-10]

The amount of HRV we have over a 24-hour period is related to our age, with younger people having higher levels than those who are older.[11] The HRV for someone in their twenties will typically vary around 20 beats per minute (BPM) while at rest, while someone in their seventies would tend to have a natural variability of less than 10 BPM while at rest. You can see in the graph in Figure 1 that the HRV amplitude is varying from around 60 BPM to around 90 BPM, but the average heart rate is around 75 BPM. Having a lower range or amount of HRV than is normal for your age is a predictor of future health problems and is associated with numerous medical conditions.

It's well known that our perceptions and emotions can cause changes in the activity of our nervous system that can affect our heart, such as when something startles us and we feel our heart rate increase. But it's not commonly understood that the signals the heart sends to the brain flow all the way into the higher centers of the brain and can have a profound influence on our higher level mental functions. For example, the heart's HRV signals affect the activity in the cortex, which is the part of the brain that governs our thinking and reasoning capacities. You can think of HRV as a type of complex Morse code that the heart uses to communicate with the brain and body.

In our lab during the early 1990s we conducted research on activity patterns associated with various emotional states. We measured people's hormones, immune system markers, brain waves, skin conductance, muscle activity, and of course heart activity using the electrocardiogram (ECG).[12-15] At that time there were very few scientific publications on positive emotions. It was through a lot of trial and error and some willing study participants, along with Doc's encouragement to have people focus on the heart and evoke warm-hearted positive feelings, like appreciation and compassion, that we observed how emotions changed the *patterns* of the heart's rhythm. We were able to publish our findings in *The American Journal of Cardiology*, and as far as we know, this was the first time that emotional states were linked to HRV patterns.[16]

Another important observation was that changes in the heart's rhythmic pattern were independent of heart rate (how many times a minute your heart beats). In fact, we can have a coherent or incoherent HRV pattern at a high or low heart rate. In other words, *it is the pattern or rhythm of our changing beat-to-beat heart rate, rather than the heart rate itself, that is reflective of our emotional state and of how harmoniously our internal systems, including our brain, are operating.* This means that from a physiological perspective, a heart-coherent state is fundamentally different than a state of relaxation, which requires only a lowered heart rate and not necessarily a coherent rhythm.

When our HRV is in a heart-coherent pattern, it reflects increased *synchronization in the communication among the neurons in our higher-level brain centers* and in the activity occurring in the two branches of the autonomic nervous system.

Heart Rhythms (Heart Rate Variability)

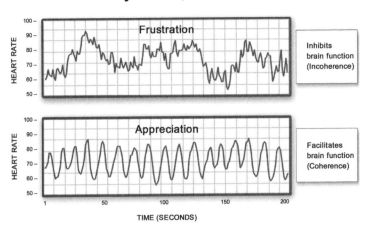

Figure 2 - The two HRV recordings shown are from the same person taken just moments apart. Emotions such as frustration, impatience, or anxiety are reflected in an incoherent heart rhythm pattern (top). The bottom, coherent, heart rhythm pattern quickly emerged when the person used HeartMath's Quick Coherence technique and activated a feeling of appreciation. In general, any regenerative emotion such as gratitude, care, compassion, or kindness tends to create more coherent heart rhythms.

When our HRV pattern is jagged and disordered, as in the top graph of Figure 2, it's called an incoherent waveform. We found that when people were experiencing stressful emotions such as frustration, anxiety, anger, fear, or worry, a disordered, incoherent heart rhythm pattern was generated.[6] On the other hand, when people were feeling sincere regenerative emotions such as love, appreciation, and compassion, their heart rhythm pattern naturally became more coherent. A smooth sine-wave-like HRV pattern as seen on the bottom graph of Figure 2 is called a coherent wave form. More technically speaking, heart coherence (also referred to as physiological coherence, cardiac coherence, or resonance) is when the HRV pattern becomes more sine-wave-like and is oscillating at a frequency of around 0.1 hertz (a 10-second rhythm), which is the natural resonant frequency of the communication system between the heart and brain.

Benefits of Coherence

Through our continued research at HeartMath Institute, we found that many beneficial things happen inside the body as we practice being in a more coherent state. Just being in a heart-coherent state for a couple of minutes has been found to lower mean blood pressure by an average of 10 points in people with high blood pressure.[17] While in a coherent state we often experience a distinct quieting of the inner "noise" generated by the normal stream of unregulated mental chatter and the replaying of stressful emotions. We have a greater sense of alignment and harmony, as well as connection with our heart's intuitive feelings or inner voice.

Have you ever noticed when you are emotionally upset that you have an increased tendency to say or do something you later regret? That's because feelings like anxiety, worry, and fear create a type of incoherence in the nervous system and brain, resulting in what's called "cortical inhibition" where we are not as able to perceive the future consequences that our reactions and resulting words or actions may have in creating stress, energy drain, and time waste. In other words, we lose our ability of foresight as our higher mental functions are taken offline![6, 7]

A growing number of research studies have shown that we can "take charge" of how we respond moment-to-moment. We can learn to better self-regulate our thoughts and emotions, which reduces and prevents many stress-producing reactions. We can do this by learning how to *intentionally shift into the state of heart coherence right in the heat of the moment*.[10, 18, 19] This creates alignment between the heart and brain resulting in "cortical facilitation," which increases our higher order capacity for mental clarity and intuitive discernment—*heart intelligence*.

Research shows that increasing our heart rhythm coherence also increases emotional flexibility and adaptability, memory, and our ability to focus and concentrate.[6, 20] As we gain more skill in self-regulating our mental and emotional energy expenditures and responses, we increase our resilience, and can improve our health and well-being relatively quickly. A simple self-regulation technique that can be used to increase heart rhythm coherence is called the Quick Coherence® technique. Many people report how effective this one-minute heart-focused breathing and emotion-shifting technique has been for them in quickly recouping from challenging situations. Try it for yourself and be your own self-scientist.

Quick Coherence® Technique

Step 1: Focus your attention in the area of the heart. Imagine your breath is flowing in and out of your heart or chest area, breathing a little slower and deeper than usual. Find an easy rhythm that's comfortable.

Suggestion: Inhale five seconds, exhale five seconds (or whatever rhythm is comfortable). Putting your attention around the heart area helps you center and get coherent.

Step 2: As you continue heart-focused breathing, make a sincere attempt to experience a regenerative feeling such as appreciation or care for someone or something in your life.

Suggestion: Try to re-experience the feeling you have for someone you love, a pet, a time in nature or a special place, an accomplishment, etc., or focus on a feeling of calm or ease.

Establishing a New Baseline

There is a direct neural pathway from the heart to a key brain center involved in processing emotion called the amygdala. In fact, the cells at the core of the amygdala synchronize to the heartbeat. In other words, the heart rhythm pattern is informing the amygdala with important information that helps determine our emotional state. Incoherent heart rhythms can be interpreted by the amygdala as anger, anxiety, or another stressful feeling, while coherent rhythms are interpreted by the amygdala as everything is okay. However, for this process to work, the amygdala needs a baseline or reference to compare the heart's incoming signals to. For example, if you're anxious a lot, then anxiety can become a familiar pattern (baseline) and feel normal. This is how a stress habit is created.

Familiar and unproductive emotional habits, such as quick trigger reactions, getting angry, being anxious, blaming, etc., can be reprogrammed as we practice getting in a heart-coherent state. This state allows for increased cellular acceptance of new and beneficial patterns instated by conscious intention. This is because of the harmonious alignment that coherence creates between the heart, mind, emotions, and nervous system.

We can learn to sustain coherence for longer periods, such as during heart meditations, to more quickly establish a healthier new baseline pattern. This creates a new inner reference or set-point that replaces the old ineffective emotional pattern. Without establishing a new baseline, it's nearly impossible to sustain a desired mental, emotional or behavioral change. Increasing the coherent alignment between our heart, mind, and emotions strengthens our capacity to change ineffective behaviors and habits that have been holding us back from accessing our higher potentials.

Assistive Coherence Feedback Technology

We also found that enabling people to see HRV patterns in real time proved to be a powerful demonstration of how emotions, such as frustration and impatience, affect the activity in their nervous system—and how quickly people can shift into a coherent state once they know how. It was not long after publishing this research that Heart-Math staff who delivered training programs in hospitals, schools, and companies wanted to include a "live HRV demo" in their programs. These live demonstrations were a hit. However, the equipment was cumbersome to use; electrodes had to be stuck on the participants' chests, and our trainers needed an extra padded suitcase to transport this rather expensive lab equipment to the venue.

It became clear that the ability to see their heart rhythm pattern before and after using a HeartMath technique to shift into a coherent state, was an "ah-ha" moment for most of the participants, and it accelerated their learning and practice of the coherence techniques. So we decided to see if we could create a low cost HRV coherence feedback device that anyone could use in everyday life. To do this we also needed to develop a way to quantify or measure coherent and incoherent states. It took some time, a lot of testing and trial and error, but we were eventually able to assess different levels of coherence. This was an important step in being able to design a user-friendly coherence training device. We worked with a team of software and hardware developers to create the first-ever consumer friendly HRV coherence feedback device in 1999, which was called the Freeze-Framer (named after the Freeze Frame® Technique, which we teach in our training programs).

Doc guided the development of some simple, short interactive games that are controlled by the user's emotional state or level of coherence to make coherence training more fun for teenagers as well as adults. At that time we had no idea we were launching what would become a new industry. At first, we wondered if anyone would buy this new computer software and sensor. But fortunately the Freeze-Framer was quickly embraced by the biofeedback industry, many healthcare professionals, business executives, golfers, and even teachers for their classrooms. A few years later it was renamed the emWave and a handheld emWave was also developed. Then sensors for iOS and Android mobile devices were developed for the Inner Balance Trainer app, Global Coherence app, and other apps.

HeartMath coherence sensors and apps are now used by hundreds of thousands of people as training tools to increase their heart rhythm coherence when practicing HeartMath or other techniques. The real-time feedback has proven to be effective for helping people sustain coherence for longer periods and increase the *carryover effect* of coherent alignment into their daily activities. Sustaining coherence facilitates the process of establishing a healthy new baseline by progressively resetting the heart's rhythms to a more coherent and resonant state.

Many people who use our technology during meditation have told me that coherence feedback helps them quickly access a meditative state, and signals them when they lose focus so they can shift back into a heart-coherent state. I have found that coherence feedback especially helps people learn *how* to slow their mental/emotional vibratory rate so that their internal systems can operate more in sync, which creates a stronger connection with their heart's intuitive guidance.

Coherent Heart Power

There's a big pay-off from practicing heart coherence for even a few minutes. As we have said, being in a coherent state has a *carryover effect*.[6] This means that by spending a few minutes in a more heart-coherent state before engaging in situations that may be stressful, such as before an important meeting or a challenging conversation with a family member, client or coworker, we are more likely to be able to sustain our inner balance and composure.

When we sit quietly in a heart-coherent state, it can at times seem like not much is going on; yet from a physio-logical view, a lot is going on. When you're in a coherent state, your nervous system is more aligned, your hormon-al and immune systems are getting rebalanced, and your mind and emotions are connecting with more of your spirit. All of this internal realignment increases resilience throughout your system.

As we increase our personal heart coherence baseline, it also benefits our families, coworkers, friends, and more. From our research, we know that heart coherence is not an idle state; it reaches out, influences, and supports others in many beneficial ways and expands into social coherence. Creating a healthy heart coherence baseline, personally and collectively, can provide people with more intuitive connectivity and flow, supporting behavior changes we want to make, and enabling new solutions for our personal and societal challenges.

Notes

1. Ho, M.-W., *The Rainbow and the Worm: The Physics of Organisms,*2005, *Singapore: World Scientific Publishing Co.*

2. Damasio, A., *Looking for Spinoza: Joy, Sorrow, and the Feeling Brain,* 2003, Orlando: Harcourt.

3. Armour, J.A., *Potential clinical relevance of the 'little brain' on the mammalian heart. Exp Physiol*, 2008. **93**(2): p. 165-76.

4. Velden, M. and M. Juris, *Perceptual performance as a function of intra-cycle cardiac activity. Psychophysiology*, 1975. **12**(6): p. 685-92.

5. Lacey, J.I. and B.C. Lacey, *Two-way communication between the heart and the brain: Significance of time within the cardiac cycle. American Psychologist*, 1978(February): p. 99- 113.

6. McCraty, R., Atkinson, M., Tomasino, D., & Bradley, R. T, *The coherent heart: Heart-brain interactions, psychophysiological coherence, and the emergence of system-wide order. Integral Review*, 2009. **5**(2): p. 10-115.

7. McCraty, R. and F. Shaffer, *Heart Rate Variability: New Perspectives on Physiological Mechanisms, Assessment of Self-regulatory Capacity, and Health Risk. Glob Adv Health Med*, 2015. **4**(1): p. 46-61.

8. Cameron, O.G., *Visceral Sensory Neuroscience: Interception,* 2002, New York: Oxford University Press.

9. Segerstrom, S.C. and L.S. Nes, *Heart rate variability reflects self-regulatory strength, effort, and fatigue. Psychol Sci*, 2007. **18**(3): p. 275-81.

10. McCraty, R. and M. Zayas, *Cardiac coherence, self-regulation, autonomic stability, and psychosocial well-being. Frontiers in Psychology*, 2014. **5**(September): p. 1-13.

11. Umetani, K., et al., *Twenty-four hour time domain heart rate variability and heart rate: relations to age and gender over nine decades. J Am Coll Cardiol*, 1998. **31**(3): p. 593-601.

12. McCraty, R., et al., *Music enhances the effect of positive emotional states on salivary IgA. Stress Medicine*, 1996. **12**(3): p. 167-175.

13. McCraty, R., M. Atkinson, and W.A. Tiller, *New electrophysiological correlates associated with intentional heart focus. Subtle Energies*, 1995. **4**(3): p. 251-268.

14. McCraty, R., et al., *The impact of a new emotional self-management program on stress, emotions, heart rate variability, DHEA and cortisol. Integr Physiol Behav Sci*, 1998. **33**(2): p. 151-70.

15. Tiller, W.A., R. McCraty, and M. Atkinson, *Cardiac coherence: a new, noninvasive measure of autonomic nervous system order. Altern Ther Health Med*, 1996. **2**(1): p. 52-65.

16. McCraty, R., et al., *The effects of emotions on short-term power spectrum analysis of heart rate variability. Am J Cardiol*, 1995. **76**(14): p. 1089-93.

17. Alabdulgader, A., *Coherence: A Novel Nonpharmacological Modality for Lowering Blood Pressure in Hypertensive Patients. Global Advances in Health and Medicne*, 2012. **1**(2): p. 54-62.

18. McCraty, R. and M. Atkinson, *Resilence Training Program Reduces Physiological and Psychological Stress in Police Officers. Global Advances in Health and Medicine*, 2012. **1**(5): p. 44-66.

19. Ginsberg, J.P., Berry, M.E., Powell, D.A., *Cardiac Coherence and PTSD in Combat Veterans. Alternative Therapies in Health and Medicine*, 2010. **16**(4): p. 52-60.

20. Lloyd, A., Brett, D., Wesnes, K., *Coherence Training Improves Cognitive Functions and Behavior In Children with ADHD. Alternative Therapies in Health and Medicine*, 2010. **16**(4): p. 34-42.

CHAPTER 11

SOCIAL COHERENCE:
LEARNING TO GET ALONG

By Howard Martin

When I was a young man in the 1970s I remember driving into Washington DC from Northern Virginia. All around me were high-rise apartments that extended for miles and miles. I imagined all the people inside and wondered, like many others: *How can so many adults and children develop a new consciousness or way of thinking needed to solve our mounting personal and social problems? How can we all get along, and allow for differences without creating separation?*

Some people become more accepting of each other's differences as they mature, often through the "school of hard knocks." But this growth process is too slow to meet the increasing challenges our world is facing. As I continued to pass the forest of buildings, I also wondered: *What if the changes each person makes contribute to an overall energetic field of consciousness that we all draw from to co-create our reality—what if there is some way we can positively contribute to that energy field that will make it easier for others to make positive changes?* Back then I didn't have a scientific understanding to verify the correctness of my feeling, but today, I have a lot to draw from.

The Energetic Field

Fast-forward twenty years. In 1996 HeartMath researchers discovered that when an individual is in a state of heart rhythm coherence their heart radiates a more coherent electromagnetic signal into the environment that can be detected by and affect the nervous systems of other people and even animals. It wasn't surprising to learn that the heart generates the strongest magnetic field in the body, approximately 100 times stronger than that produced by the brain. This energetic field can be detected several feet from the body with sensitive magnetometers. The heart's electromagnetic field provides a plausible mechanism for how we can "feel" or sense another person's presence and emotional state independent of body language or other factors.[1]

It was confirming to me when a later study examined whether people trained in heart rhythm coherence could energetically increase coherence in other people who were in close proximity but not touching. This study found that the heart coherence of an untrained participant was indeed facilitated by others who were in a coherent state. It also provided evidence of heart rhythm synchronization between people, or what is called social coherence.[2] Here's a brief summary of that study:

Forty participants were divided into 10 groups of four people who were seated around a table. They were all connected to equipment that simultaneously measured their level of heart rhythm coherence. Three of the participants had been trained in the Heart Lock-In technique and were instructed to get into a coherent state, unknown by the fourth untrained person. *Overall, as the coherent vibration of the three HeartMath-trained participants increased, the untrained person's coherence level also measurably increased just from being in that more coherent field environment.* It was as though the untrained subject had become energetically lifted into heart coherence. In addition, there was a statistical relationship between their heart rhythm synchronization and the feeling of emotional bonding among the participants.

A More Coherent Society

In social science terminology, social coherence is reflected as a stable, harmonious alignment of relationships that allows for the efficient flow of energy and communication. Social coherence can grow in a family, group, or organization in which a network of relationships exists among individuals. Social coherence requires that group members be attuned and emotionally aligned, and that the group's energy be regulated by care, not by threat or force from others. For example, in a coherent team, there is freedom for individual members to do their part and thrive while maintaining cohesion and resonance within the group's intent and goals.[3]

Many researchers are interested these days in understanding energetic social dynamics. Sociologist Raymond Bradley in collaboration with the late neuroscientist Karl Pribram developed a general theory of social communication to explain the patterns of social organization common to most groups. Bradley and Pribram found that most high-functioning groups have a global organization and coherent network of emotional energetic relations interconnecting virtually all members. They found that positive energy is required to shift a system into a more coherent mode, and *that the key to creating stable, coherent groups is related to increasing positive emotions and dissipating negative emotional tensions, interpersonal conflicts, and other stressors within and among the individuals in that group.*[4]

A growing body of evidence is suggesting that an energetic field can form between individuals in a group through which communication among all the group members occurs. In other words, there is a literal group energetic field that connects all the members. As more individuals within a group (sports team, workplace, school classroom, social group, etc.) increase their heart coherence, the group increases in social coherence and can achieve its objectives more harmoniously with more effective outcomes.[3]

In their paper *Social Baseline Theory: The Role of Social Proximity in Emotion and Economy of Action*, Drs. Lane Beckles and James A. Coan from the University of Virginia documented the benefits of emotionally-connected interactions between people.[5] I found one aspect of their work particularly fascinating with regard to the energetic influence we can have on one another's perceptions.

They wrote: *The brain modifies sensory perception in ways that bias decision-making to manage energy use efficiently.*[6] For example, wearing a heavy backpack makes distances seem further away and uphill inclines seem steeper.[7] In work by Twedt, Hawkins, and Profitt, hill slants were judged as less steep when participants stood next to a friend.[8] Moreover, this effect was moderated by the duration of the friendship—the longer the friendship, the less steep the hill.

In essence what they are describing is that our perception of walking uphill is different when we are in emotional resonance with someone. The deeper the emotional connection, the less steep the hill appears. I have found this true in my life. Most weekends I hike with a group of friends in the Santa Cruz Mountains. The hills seem much higher and hiking a lot harder when I'm by myself. What I take from this is that life gets easier and we can better achieve our goals as we develop heart-based relationships.

Some may ask, "What about negative social coherence? Isn't there a lot of emotional resonance within fanatical groups or movements that seek to dominate or impose their beliefs on others?" When a group's emotional bonding is motivated by the desire to inflict mental, emotional, or physical harm on others, they are resonating in a lower-vibrational intention that doesn't include the heart's inclusive care. The heart's intelligence by its very nature is inclusive, and heart coherence activates higher centers of the brain that experience empathy, compassion, and the desire to help others develop their higher potentials. *Social coherence* enables a "collective intelligence" that helps raise the vibratory rate of the individual's and the group's energetic field.

MIT Sloan School of Management professor Dr. C. Otto Scharmer describes collective intelligence as going from ego-system to eco-system as groups evolve towards a higher order of harmony and quality. He offers "U Theory" as the capacity for people to get along and work together. "U" theorists and researchers Joseph Jaworski and Jane Corbett find that this can be deepened through practice of heart-based awareness tools. Corbett writes, "Collective intelligence can be rapidly activated to share insights and crystallize future possibilities, even in previously stuck situations, and then take skillful action in prototyping and embedding change."[9]

In today's society there is often a surface-level harmony where people are basically civil and co-operative. That is of course important and has led to a global society that has order. However, in most groups, large or small, many individuals understandably have anxieties, judgments, frustrations, biases, and preconceptions of each other or of other groups. These feelings, said or unsaid, are energetically communicated and create separations or "closed hearts" that result in miscommunications, relational problems, and not getting along with each other.[3]

Social coherence is increasing in some groups and is needed more than ever as planetary changes are accelerating. However, it often takes a significant event for larger numbers of people to collectively open their hearts. For example, often we see an increase in social coherence after a tragedy. Events such as natural disasters tend to open people's hearts, bring people together, and lead them to put aside their differences to work cooperatively and benefit the community. Then as time passes and normalcy returns, the community spirit that was ignited by a dramatic event usually fades, as people revert to their familiar, operational baselines. Yet, many people are amazed at what they were able to accomplish together and the lasting friendships and bonds they forged.

"Lessons from Geese"

I'd like to share an analogy about the benefits that come from learning to work together. You have probably seen geese flying together in formation. It's a beautiful sight and it has a purpose. As each goose flaps its wings, it creates an uplift for the birds that follow. By flying in a V mformation, the whole flock has a 70 percent greater flying range than if each bird flew alone.

Because it's more efficient to fly this way, when a goose falls out of formation, it suddenly feels the drag and resistance of flying alone, and quickly moves back into formation.

Here is another important key to how this efficiency is created. Geese make the effort to help each other.

When the lead goose tires, it rotates back into the formation and another goose flies to the point position.

The geese flying in formation honk to encourage those up front to keep up their speed. Lastly, when a goose gets sick, two geese drop out of formation and follow it down to help protect it. They stay with it until it is able to fly again. Then, they join another formation or catch up with the flock.

There is a lot that we can learn from observing this exquisite, natural behavior of social coherence. The bottom line is this: As groups of people make efforts to increase their social coherence, this momentum can quicken the positive, evolutionary change to help society reshape itself.

Emergence of Social Coherence

An indicator of emerging social coherence can be seen today by observing the ways some large brands are shifting their marketing focus away from themselves and onto the positive contribution they can make in the world. Many companies are becoming more purpose-driven and adopting social causes because more customers want that now. It's increasingly important to millennials and younger people that businesses help to better society. We all stand to benefit from this unfolding awareness. Sure there's a lot more to be done, but we need to appreciate the steps some companies are taking, and appreciate ourselves for the steps we're taking to upgrade our personal behaviors as well.

Developing a more heart-based approach to business is also becoming more important to employees in today's work environments. It's slowly becoming accepted that people and teams do better (and so does the company's balance sheet) when they work in an atmosphere of care, appreciation, and cooperation rather than in fear and stress. More employees sense that there's more to who they *really* are. This feeling has increased since the pandemic, where so many lost jobs or worked from home and had time to rethink what they value and want to do with their lives. They are recognizing the difference between what they've been and the new person they're trying to be, and they want to follow their heart. As Steve Jobs said in a commencement address shortly after he was diagnosed with cancer, "Have the courage to follow your heart and intuition. They somehow already know what you truly want to become. Everything else is secondary."

These are extraordinary times. We are experiencing new openness and innovation, yet many aspects of organizational structure operate in a very dysfunctional way. The effects are seen and quantified in soaring healthcare costs, increased absenteeism, job dissatisfaction and poor decisions. It's difficult for leaders in most organizations to see how to get from where they are to where they hope to be.

Some of the immediate and practical benefits of increasing heart coherence in organizations include: better emotional self-management, more authentic communication, fewer mistakes, increased energy and productivity, more creativity and intuition, and better decision-making. A work environment where people move and flow with inner balance and warmth, and treat each other with compassion and care, is a more satisfying place to spend eight or more hours a day. In today's world of high-speed change and constant connectivity, leaders and employees need to be more heart-smart and intuitive than before to maximize potentials. We call this *business heart*. A leader with business heart knows that a strong heart and clear head are both essential.

James K. Clifton, Chairman and Chief Executive Officer of the Gallup Organization, reports that successful organizations can learn to build sustainable growth by harnessing the power of human emotions. He says that companies need to discover a new way to manage human nature and unlock human potential. This requires a more sensitive understanding of human emotion that the heart can bring to the table.

HeartMath coherence training is designed to help individuals and teams develop emotional self-regulation skills and access their heart's intuitive intelligence, with almost immediate health and performance benefits. Learning to bring heart, mind, and emotions into coherent alignment results in better decisions, increased creativity, and other performance benefits desired by most individuals and organizations. Pre- and post-Personal and Organizational Quality Assessments (POQA) used to determine the effectiveness of a training program have provided validation that increasing personal and social (team) coherence creates a higher level of individual and collective functioning and facilitates a healthier culture.

Dynamics of Coherent Teams

HeartMath has validated over a period of 30 years a number of effective practices for building coherent teams that we use in our training programs. We have found that the more responsible each team member is for their own energies, the better the principles of coherent teamwork have a chance to really work. At the HeartMath companies, we start meetings with a coherence practice, either the Quick Coherence technique in Chapter 10 or the Shift and Lift™ technique given on page 199. During the meeting we reset with the technique if the discussion gets incoherent or if a conflict arises. We do this because it's practical energy maintenance, especially when talking about important or sensitive issues.

Here are three of our key principles.

1. Use a coherence technique together at the start of meetings and as needed to reset the team energy for deeper listening and better communication.

2. Respect differences in opinions, backgrounds, cultures, genders, etc. Use a coherence technique to replace judgmental reactions with compassionate latitude for others and for yourself.

3. Establish a safe environment to encourage vulnerability, new ideas, admitting mistakes, and openness to questions.

A key practice is for members to deeply listen to each other without judging, which means temporarily setting their point of view aside as they listen. Practicing this sets a tone or vibration within the team that encourages psychological safety and sincere communication. This creates a more coherent energetic environment that facilitates more ease and flow in communications and creative solutions.

Here is the Shift and Lift Technique you can try. Heart-Math trainers have found this team-building technique very helpful for releasing feelings of separation and building coherence between people from diverse backgrounds and walks of life. It helps support the dignity, respect, and deep listening that builds social coherence.

Shift and Lift™ Technique:

Step 1. Heart-Focused Breathing. Focus your attention in the area of the heart. Imagine your breath is flowing in and out of your heart or chest area, breathing a little slower and deeper than usual. Find an easy rhythm that's comfortable.

Step 2. Activate feelings of kindness, appreciation, genuine connection, and an attitude of deep listening.

Suggestion: If you can't connect with a heart feeling, try to recall a time when you felt a kind, deeper connection with someone. If that is challenging, just breathe appreciation for something for awhile to help raise your vibration and to help settle your energies.

Step 3. Radiate these heart qualities to raise your vibration and help lift the energy field environment that surrounds you.

What follows are some results from over 14,000 pre- and post-psychometric POQA assessments from different industries that offer a picture of the possibilities when individuals, teams, and organizations make personal and social coherence a priority. These pre- and post-assessments reveal a consistent causal relationship between mental and emotional stress, physical stress symptoms, and organizational well-being and productivity.

Five Global Companies

In a large study conducted in five different global companies in Europe and the US, coherence training produced some significant results in personal and workplace coherence. The composite data from pre- and post-psychometric assessments of over 5,700 individuals found that, in just six to nine weeks, practicing HeartMath coherence tools produced the following average outcomes in people who reported having these symptoms *often to always*:

44% drop in fatigue; 52% drop in anxiety; 60% drop in anger; 60% drop in depression; 33% improvement in sleep.

There were also improvements in physical health in people who reported having these symptoms *often to always*:

44% drop in body aches and pains; 43% reduction in indigestion; 63% reduction in rapid heartbeats; and 44% drop in muscle tension.

Post-assessments done again after six months and then again after one year by some of the organizations showed sustained improvements.

Participants also reported a significant decrease in overwhelm and intent to leave their job. What was interesting to me is that one company manager told us that some employees continued to practice the tools they learned while many others didn't. (That would be a typical response to any training program.) Nevertheless, improvements continued and were sustained across the entire population of participants.

Other company managers/leaders commented that something in the overall energetic environment changed through the efforts made by only a portion of the people, which made it easier for others to achieve the positive benefits. This intriguing finding conveys the potential of social coherence and seems to confirm what was observed in the study mentioned at the start of this chapter where the heart rhythm coherence of three people facilitated an unconscious shift into heart rhythm coherence in a fourth person sitting around a table. The prospect of a *social coherence multiplier effect* is exciting to organizations that want to create a healthier and more caring culture.

Healthcare Systems

Hospitals and healthcare organizations have been early adopters of our programs, which isn't surprising since healthcare workers are deeply aware of the relationship between health and costs. This chart shows a meta-analysis of over 8,700 healthcare workers from several healthcare systems pre- and post-HeartMath training.

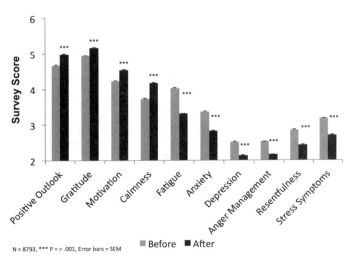

Meta Analysis of 8,793 Health Care Workers

N = 8793, *** P = > .001, Error bars = SEM

Note the statistically significant improvements in emotional states and stress symptoms.

As hospital leaders and staff learned HeartMath tools to transform stress and increase resilience, this also facilitated a shift to a more caring culture that permeated the hospital, increasing patient satisfaction. Here is one story.

Fairfield Medical Center (FMC) in Lancaster, Ohio, implemented HeartMath as an organization-wide initiative to improve quality of life for staff and quality of care for patients. To achieve FMC's enduring social mission *to be a hospital of excellence, caring for staff, patients and the community*, this 2,000+ strong team of healthcare providers adopted the HeartMath approach *to provide efficient, compassionate, safe, high-quality healthcare for FMC patients and their families.*

Cynthia Pearsall, Chief Nursing Officer at Fairfield Medical Center and a HeartMath certified trainer describes how this works. "When you feel stressed," she explains "you can literally flip the switch anytime, anyplace, into the 'stress free zone' by changing the instant message the heart sends to the brain by way of the nervous system. I start every day with a HeartMath technique called 'Heart

Lock-In' to strengthen my ability to sustain a coherent state, to achieve balance, and synchronization between my heart and mind, and to become more resilient to the stresses I am sure to face throughout the day. I even begin all of my meetings this way, with a 90-second Heart Lock-In; and if we are having a difficult time reaching a decision as a team, I will ask each of us to take a couple minutes to practice some easy coherence steps to change the quality of the moment. Once the meeting resumes, we can reliably reach a decision. HeartMath is bringing this family of caregivers, indeed this local community, closer together."

We originally thought each hospital or organization may be different in terms of the benefits achieved from coherence practice, or that different job descriptions would be affected differently. But what the research consistently shows over years is that almost any person, regardless of job or title, benefits as they and their work team practice heart coherence. And whenever a team cultivates more coherence, it has benefits for the whole organization.

For example, Kaiser Permanente Northern California trained their 21 chief nursing officers in HeartMath techniques. Their results on a normed and validated assessment showed over a 50 percent decrease in scales of fatigue, exhaustion, and anxiety, leading to over a 50 percent increase in being peaceful and calm. This directly resulted in less body aches, muscle tension, and headaches, as well as reduced power struggles, conflicts, and intention to quit the job. Similar results occurred with their medical surgical staff and nursing units. After a key medical surgical unit practiced coherence tools for three weeks, they reported a 55 percent increase in rapport strength with their supervisor and a 36 percent decrease in tension between management and staff.

Educational Outcomes

Another area where we have seen benefits from increased individual and social coherence is in educational environments. A controlled study funded by the US Department of Education that involved approximately 1,000 tenth-grade students practicing HeartMath techniques along with heart rhythm coherence technology resulted in a significant *coherence baseline* increase after just four months.[10] The experimental group was taught "TestEdge®," a HeartMath program to reduce test anxiety and improve academic test scores.

The graph below shows the physiological changes in baseline coherence in two students before and four months after training that reflected the findings of the overall group. These coherence baseline changes correlated with reduced test anxiety, improved test scores, and increased ability to get along with each other.

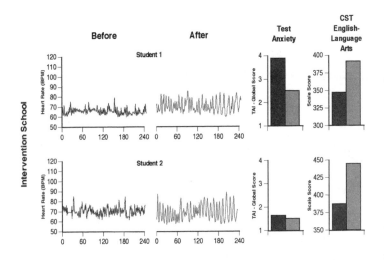

Prior to the TestEdge program, 61 percent of students reported being affected by test anxiety, with 26 percent experiencing high levels of test anxiety often or most of the time. Those with high levels of test anxiety scored an average of 15 points lower on standardized tests in both mathematics and English-language arts than students with low test anxiety. Of the students who reported being affected by test anxiety at the start of the TestEdge program, 75 percent had reduced levels of test anxiety by the end of the study.

The reduction in test anxiety in the HeartMath trained group also correlated with improvements in socio-emotional and behavioral measures: Reduction in *negative affect* (feelings of stress, anger, disappointment, sadness, depression, and loneliness); reduction in *emotional discord* (reflecting increased emotional awareness and improved emotional management); reduction in *interactional challenges* (reflecting increased empathy and improved relations with others). In addition, there was an increase in *positive class experience* (reflecting perception of increased enjoyment and learning in class, positive feelings towards classmates, and teacher care). Finally, there was also a significant increase in academic test scores in the HeartMath trained group over the control group, ranging on average from 10 to 25 points.

What moved me most when I reviewed these study results was that not only did test scores improve, so did social-emotional learning and positive behavioral changes. Teaching children emotional self-regulation skills and heart coherence tools to get along better will serve these young people throughout their lives.

Creating a Socially-Coherent Society

Heart connection is on the rise because people around the world are yearning for it. They are tired of the old ways of doing things—societal systems that don't work for everyone, belief systems that focus on separation and polarization, and a host of other paradigms that maintain the status quo.

It's also true that there are a tremendous amount of competing agendas in today's world, including political polarization, media misinformation, climate change, racial injustices, viruses, and wars. Human beings keep inflicting pain and trauma on each other. This is nothing new, but with our global communications systems the world's problems are often on full display. Nevertheless, there is plenty of hopeful news to consider in the midst of the perceived chaos. Many people are sensing that today's collective global stir is part of a transition towards a new consciousness based on care, cooperation, and acceptance. It's a process of a new world birthing itself in the midst of an old one. Awareness is shifting, people are changing, society is transforming, and a new collective intelligence is emerging.

Try for a moment to disengage from the chaos we see in society and think about this. What if many more people came to realize the transformative potential available within the heart of who they truly are? That what they have sensed about heart is real and not something only talked about in spiritual or philosophical terms. That by connecting with their heart's intelligent discernment, they can better manage their emotions; experience more compassion, appreciation, and love, while improving their health, relationships, and performance. What if increasingly more people unleashed the power of coherent alignment and partnership between their mind, emotions, and heart's intuitive guidance for navigating their daily interactions? What kind of socially coherent world might that be? When I think about these possibilities I see a new, different and better world coming into view where we care for each other. From the eyes of the heart, I can see all these things coming to pass.

Notes

1. McCraty, R., *The Energetic Heart: Biomagnetic Communication Within and Between People, in Bioelectromagnetic and Subtle Energy Medicine*, Second Edition, P.J. Rosch, Editor 2015.

2. Morris, S.M., *Facilitating collective coherence: Group Effects on Heart Rate Variability Coherence and Heart Rhythm Synchronization. Alternative Therapies in Health and Medicine*, 2010. **16**(4): p. 62-72.

3. McCraty, R., *Childre, D, Coherence: Bridging Personal, Social and Global Health. Alternative Therapies in Health and Medicine*, 2010. **16**(4): p. 10-24.

4. Bradley, R.T. and K.H. Pribram, *Communication and stability in social collectives. Journal of Social and Evolutionary Systems*, 1998. **21**(1): p. 29-80.

5. Beckes, L. and J.A. Coan, *Social baseline theory: The role of social proximity in emotion and economy of action. Social and Personality Psychology Compass*, 2011. **5**(12): p. 976-988.

6. Riener, C.R., et al., *An effect of mood on the perception of geographical slant. Cognition and Emotion*, 2011. **25**(1): p. 174-182.

7. Stefanucci, J.K., et al., *Distances appear different on hills. Percept Psychophys*, 2005. **67**(6): p. 1052- 1060.

8. Twedt, E., C.B. Hawkins, and D. Proffitt, *Perspective-taking changes perceived spatial layout. Journal of Vision*, 2009. **9**(8): p. 74-74.

9. Corbett, J., *In the Field and at the Heart of Presencing: Connecting Inner Transformation in Leadership with Organisational and Societal Change, in Leadership for a Healthy World: Creative Social Change*In press 2016.

10. Bradley, R.T., et al., *Emotion self-regulation, psychophysiological coherence, and test anxiety: results from an experiment using electrophysiological measures. Appl Psychophysiol Biofeedback*, 2010. **35**(4): p. 261- 83.

CHAPTER 12

GLOBAL COHERENCE:
THE PLANETARY POTENTIAL

By Deborah Rozman

As I was waking one morning and before I opened my eyes, these thoughts flooded into my consciousness: *The world needs as much care and compassion as it can get. What if we could collectively put out enough pure radiant love into the earth's energetic fields that it would create a multiplier effect or a quantum-coherence effect? What will it really take to shift the consciousness of humanity?* These thoughts stayed with me through my morning meditation as I radiated as much pure love, care, and compassion to the planet and humanity as I could.

When Sir Roger Penrose attended a conference in 1998 at the HeartMath Institute on whether quantum processes were involved in brain function, I asked him, "What is quantum coherence?" He replied, "This is when large numbers of particles can collectively cooperate in a single quantum state." I wondered if this could apply on a macro scale of people as well. Later, I read in Mae-Wan Ho's book

The Rainbow and the Worm that quantum coherence is what defines any living system. She also wrote, "A quantum-coherent state thus maximizes both global cohesion and also local freedom! Nature presents us with a deep riddle that compels us to accommodate seemingly polar opposites..." This riddle certainly describes the current state of our world. I pondered: *How does nature create global cohesion and also allow for free will?*

We learned in the last chapter that research findings show that as we practice heart coherence and radiate love and compassion, our heart generates a coherent electromagnetic wave into the local field environment that facilitates *social coherence*, whether in a home, workplace, classroom, or sitting around a table. As more individuals radiate heart coherence, it builds an energetic field that makes it easier for others to connect with their heart. So, theoretically it is possible that enough people building personal and social coherence could actually contribute to creating global coherence.

Science is beginning to acknowledge that we are all part of a vast web of connections that encompass not only life on this planet but the solar system and beyond. It is through this *energetic connectivity* that information, heart coherence, and resonance are exchanged. Let's look at how this energetic connectivity could potentially increase global coherence.

As said before, the term coherence implies order, structure, harmony—an alignment within and amongst systems—whether quantum particles, organisms, human beings, social groups, planets, or galaxies. This harmonious order signifies a coherent system whose optimal functioning is directly related to the ease and flow in its processes.[1]

The inner state of heart coherence is what a lot of meditation techniques (often unknowingly) attempt to achieve. There are thousands of groups and organizations all around the world using various forms of meditation or prayer to energetically help make things easier for others. Many organizations conduct synchronized meditations, prayers, intention experiments, and so forth to facilitate healing or to create a more harmonious world. Numerous studies have shown that group or collective meditation, prayer, and focused intention directed towards a specific positive outcome can have increased beneficial and measurable effects.

For example, a study conducted in 1993 in Washington DC, showed a 25 percent drop in crime rate when 2,500 meditators meditated during specific periods of time with that intention, which means that a relatively small group of a few thousand was able to influence a much larger group—a million and a half.[2] The question was then posed if crime rates could be decreased, could a group of meditators also affect social conflicts and wars? A similar experiment was done during the peak of the Israel–Lebanon war in the 1980s. Drs. Charles Alexander and John Davies at Harvard University organized groups of experienced meditators in Jerusalem, Yugoslavia, and the United States to meditate and focus attention on the area at various intervals over a 27-month period. After adjusting for variant influences, such as weather changes, Lebanese, Muslim, Christian and Jewish holidays, police activity, fluctuation in group sizes, etc., during the course of the study, the levels of violence in Lebanon decreased between 40 percent and 80 percent each time one of these meditation groups was in place, with the largest reductions occurring when the numbers of meditators were largest. During these periods, the average number of people killed during the war per day dropped from 12 to three, a decrease of more than 70 percent. War-related injuries fell by 68 percent and the intensity level of conflict decreased by 48 percent.[3, 4] Quantum physicist John Hagelin concluded from this research on the "Power of the Collective" that "since meditation provides an effective, scientifically proven way to dissolve individual stress and if society is composed of individuals, then it seems like common sense to use meditation to similarly diffuse societal stress."[5]

Every individual's energy affects the collective field environment. This means each person's emotions and intentions produce an energy that affects the field. Therefore, a first step in diffusing societal stress in the global field is for each of us to take personal responsibility for our own energies. We can do this by increasing our personal coherence and raising our vibratory rate, which helps us become more conscious of the thoughts, feelings, and attitudes that we are "feeding the field" each day. We have a choice in every moment to "take to heart" the importance of intentionally managing our energies. This is the free will or local freedom that can create global cohesion.

Each of us is also responsible for allowing thoughts and feelings of frustration, worry, separation, or blame to run unmanaged in our system. These attitudes and emotions keep our inner rhythms incoherent and out of sync, which has a depleting *carryover effect* on our hormonal, immune and nervous systems. Heart coherence practices and technology can assist us in quickly resetting our emotional energy and shifting into a harmonious inner rhythm. Heart coherence practices help to increase our vibratory rate and coherence baseline, so our spirit, heart, brain, and nervous system operate in sync and with increased efficiency. This *coherence carryover effect* enables us to be more conscious and intuitive at choice points—to move in a state of ease and choose our actions and responses rather than mechanically reacting and creating stress.

Through raising our vibratory rate, we become conscious that our energetic heart is coupled to a deeper part of our self. Many call this their "higher power" or their "higher capacities," which links us to a non-local quantum field of information and energy which physicist David Bohm called the "implicate order" and "undivided wholeness."[6] When we are in heart coherence, we have a tighter alignment with the heart intelligence that connects us to that source.

The Global Coherence Initiative

In 2008 the HeartMath Institute launched the Global Coherence Initiative (GCI). GCI is an international cooperative effort to help activate the heart of humanity and facilitate a shift in global consciousness. I am honored to be a member of the Global Coherence Initiative Steering Committee and to contribute to this vision. GCI has three primary focuses. The first is to invite people to participate by actively practicing heart coherence and adding more coherent love, care, and compassion into the planetary field. The second is scientific research on how we are energetically interconnected with each other and the earth; and the third is to educate people on how we can utilize this interconnectivity to more quickly raise our personal and collective vibratory rate to create a better world.

Here are some hypotheses that guide GCI's ongoing research in collaboration with other institutions:

1. The earth's magnetic fields are carriers of biologically relevant information that connects all living systems. Every person affects this global information field. Large numbers of people creating

heart-coherent states of love, appreciation, care, and compassion can generate a more coherent field environment that benefits others and helps offset the current planetary discord and incoherence.

2. There is a feedback loop between human beings and the earth's energetic/magnetic systems. Earth has several sources of magnetic fields that affect us all. Two of them are the geomagnetic field that emanates from the core of the earth, and the fields that exist between the earth and the ionosphere. These fields surround the entire planet and act as protective shields blocking out the harmful effects of solar radiation, cosmic rays, and other forms of space weather. Without these fields, life as we know it could not exist on the earth. They are part of the dynamic ecosystem of our planet.

Scientists know a lot about the earth's energetic fields, yet many mysteries remain. One thing that is clear is that solar activity and the rhythms taking place in the earth's magnetic fields have an impact on our health and behavior.[7] A large body of research has shown that numerous physiological rhythms and global collective behaviors *are not only synchronized with solar and geomagnetic activity, but that disruptions in these fields can create adverse effects on human health and behaviors.*[8-10]

When the earth's magnetic field environment is disturbed, it can cause sleep problems, mental confusion, unusual lack of energy, or a feeling of being on edge or overwhelmed for no apparent reason. (Sound familiar?) At other times, when the earth's fields are stable and certain measures of solar activity are increased, people report increased positive feelings and more creativity and inspiration.[11] This is likely due to a coupling between the human brain and the cardiovascular and nervous systems with resonating geomagnetic frequencies.

The earth and ionosphere generate a symphony of frequencies ranging from 0.01 hertz to 300 hertz. Some of these are in the exact same frequency range as those occurring in our cardiovascular system, brain, and autonomic nervous system.[7] This helps explain how fluctuations in the earth's and sun's magnetic fields can affect us. Changes in the earth's fields have been shown to affect our brain waves and heart rhythms, and have been associated with changes in memory and other tasks; athletic performance; number of reported traffic violations and accidents; mortality from heart attacks and strokes; and incidence of depression and suicide.[7] Changes in the earth's fields from high solar activity have also been linked to some of humanity's greatest flourishing of creativity and art.[12] This implies the increased solar activity is not necessarily problematic, but rather it's how we respond to and manage this increased energy.

GCI scientists suggest that because we have brain wave and heart rhythm frequencies overlapping the earth's field frequencies, we are not only receivers of biologically relevant information, but *we also feed information into the global field environment and essentially create a feedback loop with the earth's magnetic fields.*[11, 13] In fact, research is indicating that human emotions and consciousness encode information into the geomagnetic field and this encoded information is distributed globally. The earth's magnetic fields act as carrier waves for this information which influences all living systems and the collective consciousness. To further test this hypothesis and research, GCI has created a Global Coherence Monitoring System (GCMS).

Global Coherence Monitoring System (GCMS)

The GCMS is a worldwide network of ultra-sensitive magnetometers, designed to continuously measure magnetic signals that occur in the same range as human physiological frequencies, including our brainwave rhythms and heart rhythms. It is the first global network of GPS time-synchronized geomagnetic field detectors that track and measure resonances and fluctuations in the fields caused by solar storms, changes in solar wind speed, other magnetic field disruptions, and potentially, major global events that have a strong emotional component. As of this writing, there are six sensor sites: Northern New Zealand; Boulder Creek, California; Hofuf, Saudi Arabia; Alberta, Canada; Baisogala, Lithuania; and Bonamanzi Game Park, South Africa. The GCMS will eventually expand to approximately 12 sensor sites.

Each site collects continuous data that enables us to research how the fields affect human mental and emotional processes, health outcomes, and collective behaviors. GCMS technology will also enable research teams to explore how collective human emotional states, meditations, and intentions may be reflected in the earth's fields. In addition, we hope to investigate if changes in the earth's magnetic fields occur before natural catastrophes, like earthquakes and volcanic eruptions, or human events that have a strong global emotional impact, such as a social crisis or terrorist attack.

Although scientists have previously looked at some of the possible interactions between the earth's fields and human, animal, and plant activity, data coming from GCI research studies and the GCMS are showing that we may be more deeply interconnected with the earth's fields than previously thought. The figure below shows an example of the earth's field-line resonances, recorded at the GCMS site in Boulder Creek, California.

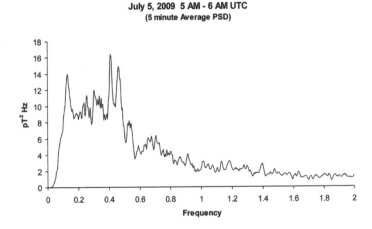

July 5, 2009 5 AM - 6 AM UTC
(5 minute Average PSD)

Figure 1 - The frequencies of these particular field-line reso-nances are in the same range as many of the rhythms found in human and animal cardiovascular and autonomic nervous-system functions. In this Boulder Creek GCMS site graph, there is a clear frequency at 0.1 hertz (the same frequency as the heart rhythm in a heart-coherent state). Most mathematical models show that the resonance frequency of the human cardiovascular system is determined by feedback loops between the heart and brain. In humans and in many animals, the resonance frequency of the system is approximately 0.1 hertz.

If the GCI hypothesis proves true, that the earth's magnetic fields are a carrier of information that connects all living systems, it will help people understand how individually and collectively we are affecting the global information field. That our attitudes, emotions, and intentions do matter and can affect all life on our planet, *and that heart-coherent, cooperative intent could impact global events and improve the quality of life on Earth.*

The hypothesis suggests that when large numbers of people respond to a global event with common emotional feeling, this collective response affects the quality of information distributed throughout the earth's field. In cases where the event evokes a negative or fearful emotional response, this can be thought of as a planetary stress wave; and in cases where a positive emotional response is evoked, it could create a planetary coherence wave. One of GCI's goals is to research whether large numbers of people generating heart-coherent states of love, care, appreciation, and compassion can build a heart-coherent field environment and a mutually beneficial feedback loop between people and the earth's fields to facilitate *global coherence*.

Interconnectivity Research

One of HeartMath Institute's interconnectivity studies involved 1,600 GCI members from countries around the world. The main goal of the study was to see if there were correlations that would indicate an interconnectedness among groups of participants located near four sites around the globe where there are GCMS sensors: Saudi Arabia, Lithuania, New Zealand, and California. Six scales were used in the study: positive affect/positive feelings, well-being, anxiety, confusion, fatigue, and physical symptoms. The study found that as solar-wind speed and polar-cap activity increased, positive affect/positive feelings and well-being decreased and anxiety, confusion, and fatigue increased.[11]

Additional studies were done with groups of participants wearing heart rate variability (HRV) recorders over long time periods to determine how the solar and earth magnetic fields affect autonomic nervous system functioning. One surprising finding was that certain solar radio changes and lower magnetic field disturbances evoked a positive nervous system response. Mental clarity increased and people felt better.

An even more surprising finding from the data was an indication that participants' heart rhythms were synchronizing at a deep level to some external signal in the earth's magnetic-field environment.[14] What we found was that participants who were thousands of miles away from each other showed synchronized HRV. One hypothesis is that the magnetic field of the earth that we all live in is somehow connecting people in sync. The magnetic field is the medium. What the data implies is that we are both receiving information from the magnetic field and feeding information into the field. The evidence suggests that what tunes us to each other in the field is emotional bonding. That the primary determinant of how in sync we are with each other regardless of distance is our emotional bonding.

We conducted another study to look more deeply at the degree of synchronization between participants' heart rhythms and the earth's magnetic field. Groups of 20–40 people in 5 countries wore HRV recorders for 15 days. All the participants (more than 100 people) practiced the Heart Lock-In technique at the same time for 15 minutes, sending love and appreciation to each other and to Earth.

When we looked at heart-to-heart synchronization between the participants, we saw that their heart rhythms were much more synchronized during and after practicing the Heart Lock-In Technique.

Our hypothesis is that over 100 hearts radiating love and appreciation into the energetic field at the same time facilitated emotional bonding or resonance. We also observed a very slow rhythm in their HRV that we hadn't seen before in research. This slow-wave rhythm was synchronizing with the rhythms in the earth's fields as measured by the GCMS. The implication of this evidence is that at some level we're connected to each other. That the resonant frequencies in the earth's fields act like carrier waves that connect us to each other through the heart, and that while in heart rhythm coherence we are in sync with the earth's fields at a slow-wave rhythm.

What is also interesting is that just 15 minutes of practicing the Heart Lock-In together at the same time appeared to *have a carryover effect that kept participants' more in sync with Earth for the next 24 hours.* There is growing evidence that there are numerous benefits of being in sync with Earth—for example, we are more intuitive and have more mental clarity. There is also preliminary evidence that if you're in a high stress state you fall out of sync with Earth.

Given that we have a stressed-out, overwhelmed, and exhausted world, perhaps getting in heart coherence and synchronization with each other and the earth's fields can boost our collective intuition, mental clarity, and overall well-being.

The planetary potential for groups of people generating heart coherence in the global information field is that it can create synchronicities and synergies that can draw in nonlocal intuition for problem-solving and addressing our social, environmental, and global stress challenges.

As Nobel Laureate Ilya Prigogine discovered in his research: *When a system is far from equilibrium, small islands of coherence in a sea of chaos have the capacity to lift the system to a higher order.*

GCI Emissaries

Tens of thousands of people from more than 150 countries have become GCI Emissaries to help co-create a better world through sending collective love and compassion into the global field environment. GCI Emissaries can join together on the Global Coherence app as they send heart-coherent energy to the planet to help raise the vibratory rate or send care and compassion to high-stress areas to help lessen people's suffering, especially during times of crisis. Due to increased disruptions, stress, and pain that many people are experiencing throughout the world, sending compassion is one of the highest forms of love we can give to help people restore and rebalance their system.

Participants on the Global Coherence app can view a global map of people at different locations using the app at the same time. Anyone can participate in the Global Coherence app and everyone's heart energy counts.

GCI Emissaries also commit to practicing heart coherence techniques to increase their coherence baseline. Because of increasing time pressures these days, GCI does not require specific time commitments. GCI Emissaries determine how much time and energy and when they can contribute to a Care Focus event or to radiate compassion and care out to the planet.

Using HeartMath's heart coherence sensor with the app is not required but is recommended for two reasons. It helps you track your coherence level and increase your personal coherence baseline which raises the community's collective coherence; it enables you to participate in GCI research studies that require objective measures of participants' coherence levels.

GCI's Emissaries Introductory Heart Coherence Technique

You can use this GCI Emissaries Heart Coherence technique to increase and sustain your personal coherence. Here are the six steps of this powerful tool:

- Breathe and calm yourself in whatever ways you choose.

- Choose something you appreciate—a person, pet, nature, etc., and radiate the feeling of appreciation to them for about two minutes. This helps open the heart more and increases your effectiveness when you start sending care to the planet or to a situation that needs it.

- Evoke genuine feelings of compassion and care for the planet.

- Breathe the feelings of compassion and care going out from your heart. *(To help with focus, some imagine their compassion and care flowing out like a river flows out to the sea. Others imagine their compassion and care radiating as a beam of light, or they radiate it out with the rhythm of their breath. Determine what is right for you.)*

- Radiate the genuine feelings of compassion and care to the planet or to a specific area of immediate need.

- See yourself joining with other caretakers to participate in the healing process and generate peace.

- *How long should you do this Heart Coherence technique?* You decide. Most practice this technique at least five minutes a day to build personal coherence. The amount of time often increases for people as they begin to understand and experience the *carryover effect* and the benefits of coherence for themselves and others. Depending on your schedule, you likely will spend more time doing the technique on some days than others.

An Iterative Process

As we increase our personal coherence, we become more sensitive to our heart's signals. When we act more often on what our heart intelligence is saying, our heart's signals get stronger and clearer. In Chapter 3 we mentioned the seminal work of John and Beatrice

Lacey on heart-brain interactions. Joseph Chilton Pearce quotes the Lacey's in his book *Evolution's End: Our brain sends a running report of our environmental situation to the heart, and the heart exhorts the brain to make a proper response.*[15] GCI's theory is that increased *individual coherence* leads to increased *social coherence*, which in turn leads to increased *global coherence* in an iterative process.

GCI Model of Transformation

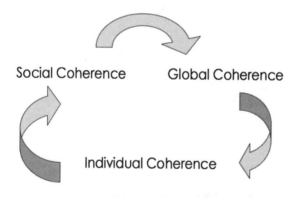

Social Coherence   Global Coherence

Individual Coherence

As the iterative process spirals up, it generates a higher-vibrational consciousness field that couples with the earth's fields to accelerate individual, social, and global coherence and resonance. If this theory proves true, it will support co-creative alliances and empower humanity as a species to serve as caretakers of our planet for generations to come. In time, global coherence will be reflected in leaders and nations adopting a more coherent global view. At this scale and from this level of consciousness, social and economic oppression, warfare, cultural intolerance, crime, and disregard for the environment can be addressed meaningfully and successfully.

As the oft-repeated quote attributed to Albert Einstein states, "No problem can be solved from the same level of consciousness that created it." Now more than ever, people are experiencing a desire to raise the vibration of their consciousness and they conveniently have all of the directions within their heart.

Coherence: A Doorway to Heart-Based Living

At HeartMath we use the phrase heart-based living as a "street" term for coherent living. The term heart-based is randomly used by many people as a generic reference to "leading with the heart" or something similar. We didn't coin the term, but we like it because it's easy to say and it casually projects its meaning.

HeartMath is only one of many systems and practices that promote aspects of heart-based or heart-centered living. There are numerous taglines and expressions which refer to living from the heart; but regardless of what label we put on it, practicing it can make a life-changing difference. Increasing our individual heart coherence can contribute to a new world of social and global coherence, based on the proven intelligence that getting along with each other is the missing piece in our ability to thrive as a planet and draw solutions for creating a world we all want to live in.

Notes

1. McCraty, R., Childre, D, *Coherence: Bridging Personal, Social and Global Health. Alternative Therapies in Health and Medicine*, 2010. **16**(4): p. 10-24.

2. Hagelin, J.S., Orme-Johnson, D. W., Rainforth, M., Cavanaugh, K., & Alexander, C. N. , *Results of the National Demonstration Project to Reduce Violent Crime and Improve Governmental Effectiveness in Washington, D.C. Social Indicators Research*, 1999. 47: p. 153-201.

3. Davies, J.L., *Alleviating political violence through enhancing coherence in collective consciousness: Impact assessment analysis of the Lebanon war. Dissertation Abstracts International*, 1988. **49**(8): p. 2381A.

4. Orme-Johnson, D.W., et al., *International Peace Project in the Middle East THE EFFECTS OF THE MAHARISHI TECHNOLOGY OF THE UNIFIED FIELD, The Journal of Conflict Resolution*, 1988. **32**(4): p. 776-812.

5. Hagelin, J., *The Power of the Collective. Shift: At the Frontier of Consciousness*, 2007. 15: p. 16-20.

6. Bohm, D., *Wholeness and the Implicate Order*, 1980, London: Routledge and Kegan Paul.

7. McCraty, R. and A. Deyhle, *The Global Coherence Initative: Investigating the Dynamic Relationship between People and Earth's Energetic Systems in Bioelectromagnetic and Subtle Energy Medicine*, Second Edition, P.J. Rosch, Editor 2015.

8. Doronin, V.N., Parfentev, V.A., Tleulin, S.Zh, Namvar, R.A., Somsikov, V.M., Drobzhev, V.I. and Chemeris, A.V., *Effect of variations of the geomagnetic field*

and solar activity on human physiological indicators.
Biofizika, 1998. **43**(4): p.647-653.

9. Kay, R.W., *Geomagnetic Storms: Association with Incidence of Depression as Measured by Hospital Admission. British Journal of Psychiatry*, 1994. 164: p. 403-409.

10. Mikulecký, M., *Solar activity, revolutions and cultural prime in the history of mankind. Neuroendocrinology Letters*, 2007. **28**(6): p. 749- 756.

11. McCraty, R. & Al Abdulgader, A. *Consciousness, The Human Heart and The Global Energetic Field Environment.* Cardiol Vasc Res 5, 1-19 (2021).

12. Ertel, S., *Cosmophysical correlations of creative activity in cultural history. Biophysics*, 1998. **43**(4): p. 696-702.

13. McCraty, R., A. Deyhle, and D. Childre, *The global coherence initiative: creating a coherent planetary standing wave. Glob Adv Health Med*, 2012. **1**(1): p. 64-77.

14. McCraty, R. et al. *Synchronization of Human Autonomic Nervous System Rhythms With Geomagnetic*

Activity in Human subjects Journal of Environmental Research and Public Health 14, 1-18, doi:10.3390/ijerph14070770 (2017).

15. Pearce, J.C., *Evolution's End 1992, New York: Harper-Collins*. P. 106

CHAPTER 13

BROADCASTING LOVE

By Doc Childre

Most of us sense that profound societal changes will continue to take place as our world becomes increasingly interconnected and interdependent. For this to achieve its potential, we need to all learn to get along. The mind without the heart hasn't been able to pull this off. The good news is this: *The dynamic shift the collective is experiencing now across the planet is creating a time-release momentum for awakening humanity to open our hearts and step our love down into kindness, compassionate care, forgiveness, cooperation, and fresh starts.*

Increasing our coherence makes cooperation and compassionate care for each other come naturally. Coherence occurs at all levels in nature, from the micro to the macro and within the human experience. Coherence is a natural state that accompanies who we are at the core of our being. While in a heart-coherent state people experience a distinct quieting of the inner "noise" generated by unregulated mental and emotional activity. They have a greater sense of alignment as well as a clearer connection to their heart's intuitive feelings and effective directions.

Heart coherence does not disesteem the mind; it increases the mind's potentials for balanced viewpoints which are more inclusive of the whole. Our basic systems (heart, mind, emotions, and body) create more harmony and fulfillment when working in cooperation to shape our lives for the better.

The practice of sitting in heart rhythm coherence for even a few minutes accumulates higher-vibrational energy that has a carryover effect through our day; it provides more clarity and ability to access flow. This often draws creative solutions where there seem to be none. In a coherent vibration we draw more synchronicities and clearer choices, along with heightened heart textures of love in our life's interactions. We don't have to be perfect without challenges to maintain a coherent life expression. It simply requires general maintenance, like any practice that helps to steer our decisions and behaviors.

Scientific research is showing that as people practice heart coherence, it generates an energetic field that makes it easier for others to connect with their heart— leading to greater understanding of each other and *social coherence*. It's our individual job to become responsible for our own energy which raises the vibration of the collective energy field, making it easier for others to access their higher potentials and increased joy.

The emerging field of interconnectivity research is exploring how this higher vibration can be amplified, creating the potential for *global coherence*. Researchers have found that when people are sincerely sending out love and compassionate care into the energetic field, it benefits their own health and the health of others. In 23 published studies on distance healing, 57 percent showed statistically significant positive psychological and biological changes associated with improved health, including lowered blood pressure, reduced stress and anxiety, increased immune response, improved hormonal balance and more positive mood states.[1]

As collective awareness increases, science and spiritual exploration will join together in partnership which will create unlimited benefits for the whole of humanity. It's time to acknowledge that powerful, life-changing positive movements are growing in the midst of the transitional chaos that the planet is going through. More people are sensing that some of the rough edges humanity is experiencing are the release of old energies that no longer serve us, which creates an opportunity to *reset our lives*. As a result of these energetic changes, people will progressively wake up and realize that we can become much more than we ever thought possible—yet we have to individually pedal some to create that ride.

To Love Is Why We Are Here

Love is an action word for achieving our next awareness level of collective intelligence. *We won't be able to sidestep genuine love, care, and compassionate interaction*. We've tried that through the ages, and it hasn't worked. Love is a core heart frequency that unifies and lifts people's perceptions above separation. When we choose to be more caring, kind, and cooperative with each other for the good of the whole, we can create self-sustaining socioeconomic ecosystems that provide the opportunity for all to prosper.

Love is a transformational intelligence that raises consciousness to a next level and draws solutions we haven't yet thought of with multiple benefits. The need for love has been philosophized for eons—and now is the time for us to take it to the street by practicing more care, kindness, patience, and compassion in our interactions.

Radiating or Sending Love

The practice of radiating or sending love while sitting in coherence helps to calm the overactive mind and emotions, which increases our ability to handle the elevated stress levels on the planet. Also, the practice of forgiving ourselves and others steps up the quality of our love and our mental, emotional, and physical healing capacity. When our heart, mind, and emotions are in coherent alignment and not in conflict with each other, this makes it easier to sense our heart's intuitive nudges for more effective choices and guidance.

There are many individual and collective benefits from the practice of intentionally broadcasting or radiating love or compassionate care. Doing this automatically brings more patience and deeper listening into our interactions. After we practice radiating love or compassionate care for a while, there's an automatic tendency to precede interactions from a more loving spirit, resulting in less stress and more harmony in our relationships. Sending love in the form of compassionate care and respect also helps to soften the energetic field around us, making it easier for others to feel ease and a deeper resonant connection in their heart.

People radiating love and compassion at the same time create a stronger heart-filled environment. This is why we see more groups creating online events for thousands to radiate love and compassion to those suffering hardships and to the planet. Millions of people participate in collective prayer, meditation, and compassion initiatives with the intention of facilitating higher outcomes. I suggest that this won't be a passing trend—it will become a commonsense practice and many more will want to participate and experience the benefits. The effectiveness of these outpourings will increase each participant's personal vibration, which does much to raise the collective consciousness. It's this higher vibration of the collective spirit that creates the benevolent outcomes—moreso than the numbers of people involved. The collective intention for HeartMath and the Global Coherence Initiative is to help bring about this transforming environment, however long it takes.

The effectiveness of collective heart power is in its early stages—yet it's on the rise due to the rapid increase of stress and a desperate need for solutions that the mind without the heart can't deliver. As people's hearts, minds, and emotions resonate in coherent alignment, this allows more spirit and heart energy to move through individual and collective intentions. More people throughout the planet will be practicing coherent alignment to unlock their higher potentials and free up the spirit of *who they truly are*. We are running out of ways trying to find happiness and peace without opening our hearts to getting along with each other. We need to find a new respect for our personal and cultural differences. *This is a job for love that can't be substituted.*

Here are some ways to increase our practice of radiating or sending love—but *remembering* to do them is what can make the difference.

Exercises to Expand Our Capacity to Love

- Make a commitment to consciously broadcast or radiate love for a minute or two in between and during activities during the day or whenever you think of it. Realize that you are especially radiating love when you're feeling appreciation and kindness, resonance with nature, warm-hearted care for family, friends, pets, etc.

- Practice breathing love and caring feelings into the environment wherever you are: shopping, on the phone, at the dinner table, watching the news, in meetings, while driving or walking to work, etc. As you do this, know that it's helping to increase your capacity for finding solutions to life's challenges.

- Sit for a while in relaxed stillness and imagine breathing love and healthy thoughts into all your cells. This enhances your immune, hormonal, and nervous systems which can help with self-healing. Remember it's been proven in respected studies that love energy can effect positive changes in biology.[2]

- Practice radiating love and latitude into future meetings or interactions you're planning. This sets a tone for deeper listening from your heart and helps you maintain or recoup emotional poise if needed.

Doing these exercises for a week or longer strengthens your inner stability, while helping to prevent stressors that block clear thinking and higher choices. It takes a little repeated practice to *remember* to do them, but it's way worth the time spent to anchor any of these practices into memory. Set up phone or note reminders. Some days you won't feel the heart as much. Heart feelings modulate at times, but that's okay. It's your sincere heart intention that increases effectiveness and for radiating love and compassionate care to become more automatic.

These exercises are intended to inspire your own creative ways to expand your heart's love and care in action and experience the transformational benefits that come with it. Your heart will start to inform you of the myriad ways that compassionate care in your interactions can be effective. Remember that any situation you send positive energy from the heart to is raising the vibration of your own system and the energetic field environment surrounding the situation.

Love, compassion, kindness, and cooperation have been sparsely represented in our collective social consciousness for too long. Let's place these transformative heart qualities on the top shelf of our toolbox as we pitch in to co-create the highest best future for the whole. Accessing our natural heart intelligence can create an energetic field of unconditional love and harmonious interaction—helping humanity to realize we are one Earth, one yard, one people. Love and caring for each other is the one thing that can bring all this together and eventually thrive.

Many of us have committed to *giving peace a chance* but peace is waiting on us to take the first responsible step: Now it's time to *give love a chance*—then peace will join us at the table for celebration.

Notes

1. Astin, J. A., Harkness, E. & Ernst, E. *The efficacy of "Distant Healing" a systematic review of randomized trials. Annals of internal medicine* **132**, 903-910 (2000).

2. Ornish, Dean, Love and Survival: *8 pathways to Intimacy and Health*, William Morrow Paperbacks, February 17, 1999

ABOUT THE AUTHORS

Doc Childre
HeartMath Founder
Chairman and Co-CEO

Doc is the founder of HeartMath and a global authority on optimizing human performance and personal effectiveness. He is a consultant to business leaders, scientists, educators, and the entertainment industry. He is the originator of the HeartMath® System: a set of practical, heart-based tools and technologies that all people can use to reduce stress, improve performance, and enhance health and well-being. He is chairman and co-CEO of HeartMath, Inc., and chairman of HeartMath Institute's Scientific Advisory Board and Global Coherence Initiative Steering Committee.

Deborah Rozman, PhD
HeartMath Inc.
President and Co-CEO

Deborah has over forty years of experience as a business executive, serial entrepreneur, psychologist, author, and educator. She has been involved with Heart-Math since its inception helping to oversee its growth. She is co-author with Doc Childre of HeartMath's Transforming Series published by New Harbinger: *Transforming Stress, Transforming Anger, Transforming Anxiety,* and *Transforming Depression*. She is a key spokesperson on HeartMath, heart intelligence, managing stress in changing times, and heart-based living.

Howard Martin
HeartMath LLC
Executive Vice President

Howard brings more than thirty years of experience in business and personal development and has been involved in the development of HeartMath's programs since its inception. He is co-author with Doc Childre of *The HeartMath Solution*, published in 2000 by Harper San Francisco. Howard is a key spokesperson, conducting many interviews each year and speaking internationally on the HeartMath approach to advance human performance, global coherence, and heart intelligence.

Rollin McCraty, PhD
HeartMath Institute
Executive Vice
President and
Director of Research

Rollin has been with HeartMath since its creation in 1991. He is a psychophysiologist and has written exten-sively and been widely published in his areas of scientific interest. He holds numerous memberships, including with the American Autonomic Society, Pavlovian Society, National Association for Psychological Science, Association for Applied Psychophysiology and Biofeedback, and Society for Scientific Exploration, and he is director of research and project coordinator of the Global Coherence Monitoring System.

ADDITIONAL RESOURCES

HeartMath Inc.

Connect with Us:

- Visit us at Heartmath.com for the latest information on all of our programs, products, and services.

- Connect with us on the monthly Add Heart® Podcast, available wherever you get your podcasts.

- Sign up for *Connections*—our monthly newsletter— at HeartMath.com.

- Join us on Facebook.com/HeartMath and Linkedin. com/company/HeartMath-LLC.

Next Steps:

Enhance Your Practice with Coherence Technology

Deepen your practice with real-time coherence feedback with the Inner Balance™ sensor and app. The app displays your heart rhythm coherence level and guides you to increase your coherence and connection with your heart's intuitive guidance. Just a few minutes of practice each day has a carryover effect for more ease and flow in your day-to-day activities. Health professionals recommend the Inner Balance to help clients manage their emotions, clear clouded thinking, and improve health. **Explore more at https://www.heartmath.com/tech/**.

The HeartMath Experience

Heart intelligence comes alive in The HeartMath Experience: a 90-minute, online, beautifully illustrated video course led by Heart Intelligence authors Howard Martin, Deborah Rozman, and Rollin McCraty. Watch them review the scientific principles of heart intelligence and be guided through five techniques for bringing heart and mind into coherent alignment so you can respond to day-to-day challenges with more ease and your heart's intuitive guidance. **Register for free at https://www. heartmath.com/experience/**.

Add Heart® Facilitator Program

The Add Heart Facilitator Program takes you into a transformational experience, providing step-by-step training in how to use the Inner Balance app and sensor, and how to share coherence with family, friends, and colleagues. **Learn more at https://www.heartmath.com/training/ add-heart-facilitator-program/**.

Go Deeper with a HeartMath® Mentor or Coach

One of the best ways to deepen your practice of heart-based living and coherence is to work with a caring HeartMath mentor/coach who can support you in using HeartMath tools in your daily life. **Find a mentor/coach at https://certified.heartmath.com/.**

Certifications:

Become Certified as a HeartMath Mentor

Help others develop their heart intelligence by becoming certified in HeartMath's Building Personal Resilience™ program. HeartMath Certified Mentors are trained and licensed to teach clients a HeartMath skill set in one-on-one or small group settings. Learn how to guide others through a step-by-step transformational process with coherence techniques that align heart, mind, and emotions and access the heart's intuitive guidance.

Become Certified as a HeartMath Workshop Trainer

If you deliver workshops inside an organization or independently, you can become a HeartMath Certified Trainer with two certifications to choose from or take sequentially.

- **The Resilience Advantage™ Certification**
  Used by major hospital systems, Fortune 500 companies, and government organizations, The Resilience Advantage certification provides an in-depth immersion into the science behind HeartMath and skill set for better managing today's pressures, improving performance, and elevating life and work experiences. **Learn more at https://www.heartmath.com/hmct/.**

- **Activating the Heart of Teams™ Certification**
  Activating the Heart of Teams: Creating a Culture Where Teams Can Thrive certification provides a HeartMath skill set for building social or team coherence. Includes a team coherence assessment. **Learn more at https://www.heartmath.com/certification/activating-the-heart-of-teams-leadership-certification/.**

Become Certified as a HeartMath® Practitioner

If you are a health professional wanting to help clients better manage stress, anxiety, and other health issues by learning emotional self-regulation skills and coherence training, we offer three programs to choose from.

Explore more at https://www.heartmath.com/health-professionals/.

- **HeartMath Clinical Certification**

  This online course teaches how to integrate HeartMath in clinical settings. Includes 20 CE credits. Technology not included.

- **HeartMath Interventions Certification**

  This online course teaches HeartMath self-regulation tools and how to use coherence technology with patients and clients. Includes the emWave® Pro Plus technology. CE credits not included.

- **The Resilient Heart™ Trauma-Sensitive Certification**

  This online course is for those who work in a therapeutic relationship with people who have experienced trauma.

To explore more of HeartMath, visit these websites:

Blog: **https://www.heartmath.com/blog/**

Solutions pages: **https://www.heartmath.com/solutions/**

How to Contact Us:

HeartMath.com

info@heartmath.com

HeartMath Inc.

14700 West Park Avenue

Boulder Creek, CA 95006

(831) 338-8700

(800) 450-9111

HeartMath Institute

A 501c3 nonprofit organization

Become a HeartMath Institute (HMI) Member

HeartMath Institute members support the research and non-profit work of HMI. You'll enjoy perks such as ebooks, scientific monographs, informative webinars exclusively for members, and unlimited access to an array of resources. You'll have easy access to free resources on your personalized My Member Page where you can stay informed and be inspired on your journey of the heart. **Learn more about becoming a member at https://www. heartmath.org/membership/.**

Donate

Your charitable gift to HeartMath Institute supports innovative research in heart rate variability (HRV), the psychophysiology of emotions, heart-brain communication and how these relate to managing stress, increasing coherence, and deepening your connection to self and others. It also enables HMI to continue two of our most exciting areas of research: the electrophysiology of intuition and the interconnectedness of people, trees, earth and all life. HMI's research has led to the Global Coherence

Initiative and to the development of effective programs and simple techniques for increasing personal, social, and global coherence and harmony. Your generosity improves the lives of children, adults, and those in need.

HeartMath Institute is a "100-percent model," meaning all contributions support research and projects that help people. **Donate at https://store.heartmath.org/Donations-GCI/Donation-to-IHM.html.**

Bring Heart Intelligence to Schools and Children

HeartMath education projects teach children how to access their heart's wisdom, which is essential for navigating these times and for heart-based living. Learning emotional self-regulation skills early in life greatly increases the likelihood of future success in school and life. Social and behavioral sciences have found that self-regulation skills underlie mental and emotional health, positive relationships, and academic success. HMI's research since 1991 is incorporated into practical tools and programs that give parents, teachers, and other educators proven methods to help children attain heart-based skills and fully engage in life. Your charitable gift to HeartMath education projects provides sponsorships for life-changing educational programs and resources to students, teachers, and those who otherwise could not access them. **Donate at https://www.heart-math.org/donations/give/education/.**

HMI's learning programs help young people learn valuable skills to do and be their best—and have lots of fun doing it!

Learn more at https://store.heartmath.org/ heartmath-school-programs/.

Resources for Heart-Coherent Parenting
Visit our Resources page for parents where you'll find many articles covering a range of topics, ideas, and tools for people who raise children. You'll also find parenting self-care resources to help you take care of your needs so you can better take care of your children's needs. **Explore these resources at https://www.heartmath.org/ resources/parenting/parenting-resources/.**

Global Coherence Initiative
Learn about the free Global Coherence App: **https:// www.heartmath.org/gci/global-coherence-app/.**

Become a Global Coherence Emissary: **https://www.heartmath.org/gci/emissary/.**

Personal Well-Being Survey

This scientifically validated survey gives you a quick but accurate overview of four key dimensions of your well-being: stress management, adaptability, resilience, and emotional vitality. At the end of the survey, you will receive suggestions on practical steps for improving your ability to more effectively neutralize stressful emotions and increase your resilience. **Take the survey at https://www. heartmath.org/resources/personal-well-being-survey/.**

Resources for Building Heart Intelligence

Explore HeartMath's collection of free resources and downloadable materials for expanding your heart connections. These include practical solutions for personal growth, health, and life fulfillment. **Learn more at https:// www.heartmath.org/resources/.**

HeartMath Institute's Road to Coherence

View this short overview video at https://www.youtube.com/watch?v=-otFYviO2zQ.

Connect with HeartMath Institute:

- Join our growing community on Facebook.com/HeartMathInstitute.

- Find us on LinkedIn at Linkedin.com/company/Institute-of-HeartMath.

- Check out our blog at https://www.heartmath.org/blog/.

How to Contact Us:

https://www.heartmath.org/

info@heartmath.org

HeartMath Institute

P.O. Box 1463

Boulder Creek, CA 95006

(800) 711-6221

(831) 338-8500